Arnt Cobbers

Erich Mendelsohn

1887 – 1953

The Analytical Visionary

TASCHEN

HONG KONG KÖLN LONDON LOS ANGELES MADRID PARIS TOKYO

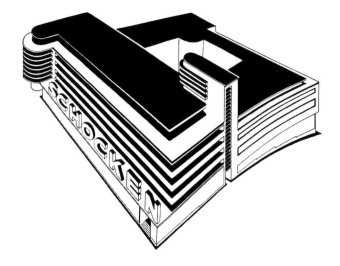

Illustration on page 2 ► Erich Mendelsohn on the
terrace of his house Am Rupenhorn in Berlin, 1931
Illustration page 4 ► Schocken Department Store
in Stuttgart, Germany, 1926 – 1928, stylized
illustration

Editor ► Peter Gössel, Bremen
Project management ► Katrin Schumann, Eike
Meyer, Bremen
Layout ► Gössel und Partner, Bremen
Text edited by ► Avinus, Berlin
Translation ► Maureen Roycroft Sommer,
Bergisch Gladbach

Printed in Germany
ISBN 978-3-8228-5595-9

Contents

Introduction

Opposite page:
Schocken Department Store Stuttgart, 1928
Sheet of sketches depicting four views.
Mendelsohn rarely sketched floor plans,
as he did for the stairway tower here.

Of all the great architects of classic Modernism, Erich Mendelsohn is the most underestimated. He was the first of the young innovators (outside the Netherlands) to begin building after the First World War – before Le Corbusier, Walter Gropius or Mies van der Rohe. He created the model Expressionist building (the Einstein Tower) and developed the single most dynamic corner in modern architecture (the Rudolf Mosse Printing and Publishing Company Building). He revolutionized department store architecture and was the first to dramatically illuminate his buildings at night. He was a founder of the *The Ring*, the most important German architects' association in the 1920s, and was one of the first architects to work internationally. And still: while the literature on Le Corbusier, Gropius or Mies fills whole shelves, there is only a small body of research on Mendelsohn.

That is surprising, but not without reason. Mendelsohn's architecture is radically subjective, while the avant-garde of his day sought "scientifically" objective solutions. Mendelsohn was decidedly individualistic. He was successful, confident – and arrogant. He was the head of the largest architectural office in Germany in the 1920s – because he had no qualms about creating economically efficient, commercially effective "architectural advertising" (Adolf Behne). He did not, on the other hand, take part in the most important architectural show in the 1920s, the Weißenhofsiedlung in Stuttgart, nor in the founding of the architects' organization CIAM. As a result, Hitchcock and Johnson treated him as a marginal figure in their exhibition on International Style at the Museum of Modern Art (MoMA) in New York in 1932, and Sigfried Giedion does not mention him at all in his epoch-making 1941 book *Space, Time and Architecture*. Even Mendelsohn's contemporaries omitted him from their "roster" of great innovators of the modern period. And yet he most definitely was one.

The major historical disruptions of the twentieth century left their mark on Mendelsohn's life and work, they affected him with full force. The work he did in England, Palestine and the USA after his emigration is generally considered weaker. It differed from his earlier buildings, although when examined more closely it is extremely interesting – and continued to develop logically, based upon fundamental principles formulated early in his life.

Mendelsohn was born into modest circumstances. On 21 March 1887 he came into the world as the fourth of five children born to a Jewish merchant and a milliner in the East Prussian regional capital of Allenstein (now Olsztyn, Poland). His mother was very musical. He attended a humanistic school, began training as a merchant in Berlin in 1906, switched to economics at the university in Munich and, as of 1908, finally settled on architecture, studying in Berlin for two years and in Munich for two years.

After receiving his degree, he attempted to establish himself as a private architect in Munich. He had already designed a chapel for the Jewish cemetery in his hometown in 1911, but this small building remained his only completed project for some time. Mendelsohn earned his living designing posters, concert programmes, shop windows and stage sets, as well as by selling his own oil paintings and prints. As the "artistic

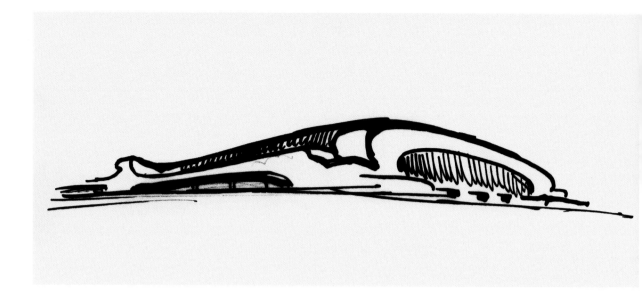

Perspectival sketch for a railway station, 1914
Pen and ink with some pencil

director" of the annual charity ball staged by the press in Munich, he designed stage sets and costumes (including two Max Reinhardt productions). In 1914 he took part in the founding of an Expressionist "artists' theatre" along with his friends the painters Kandinsky, Franz Marc and Paul Klee. The First World War precluded Mendelsohn's carrier as a stage designer.

Deferred from military service because of his poor eyesight, Mendelsohn relocated to Berlin in late 1914, where he married the 21-year-old Jewish cellist Luise Maas in 1915; eight months later their daughter, and only child, Esther was born. Mendelsohn originally met Luise Maas in 1910 – she remained the most important person in his life up to the moment of his death.

Mendelsohn never kept a diary, instead he wrote thousands of letters to his "beloved soul". The couple was, in fact, often separated, because of her concert tours and his professional commitments. The letters show Mendelsohn to be an eloquent stylist and a sharp analyst in both aesthetic and political questions – as well as very well rounded. "Whether art, economics, politics, music or philosophy: he knew so much about every subject, as if he had spent his life studying every one of them." Thus, a later description by his daughter. Asked by a student in the 1950s, which characteristics were important in order to become a good architect, Erich Mendelsohn answered by saying the primary thing was to be a "whole person".

Mendelsohn loved to philosophize at length and to express harsh criticism. But in his letters he also reveals himself to be a person of great integrity. "He never made any compromises," his daughter wrote, "but luckily his pronounced sense of humour provided some balance." Mendelsohn must have been an impressive speaker, the prose of his lectures is expressionistically brief, breathless, charged with meaning: never a word too many, staccato style.

Despite all the compromises an architect has to make, Mendelsohn saw himself as an artist – and the artist as a creator: "The will of the artist ... gives a work its uniqueness, its spirit and charm, it alone is of interest." (January 1914) And this will was absolute: "The artist carries the constants on which his work is oriented within himself,

his creativity is based on bearing witness, and never on making demands. His ultimate achievement is judged by time ... Where I go, whether stumbling through the woods, along a boulevard or on a bridle path, is beyond contemporary criticism. The tendency of my work is inevitable and cannot be alternated."

Starting in 1913, Mendelsohn began drawing sketches of visionary architectural projects without an actual commission, a site or concrete requirements, quickly dashing off drawings that formulated the essence of an idea in very few lines while simultaneously indicating the possibilities of a new building material. "Iron in combination with concrete, reinforced concrete, is the building material of the new will to form. Its structural strength capable of being loaded almost equally with stress and compression, will give rise to a new, specific logic in the laws of statics, logic of form, of harmony, of implicitness." (March 1914)

Mendelsohn almost always chose the corner perspective, depicting the building from the level of a pedestrian. It almost seems as if his fantasy buildings were frozen for a moment in mid-motion. Rhythm, energy and movement are the core concepts of Mendelsohn's architecture; he interpreted "every artistic achievement" as "outflow of a personal sense of rhythm".

Through the astrophysicist Erwin Finlay Freundlich, the client who later commissioned the Einstein Tower, he was introduced to the theory of relativity in 1914. He was fascinated by the relationship between mass and energy and applied it to architecture. "The balance of motion in mass and light – mass requires light, light moves mass – is reciprocal, parallel, complementary. Mass is clearly constructed when light balances it. Inferring back to the contour! Light is properly distributed when it balances mass in motion. Inferring back to the depiction! That is a fundamental rule of Expressionist art." (June 1917) Making the energy concealed in mass visible, uncovering the inherent dynamics – that became Mendelsohn's goal.

The fact that Mendelsohn became the leading architect in Germany after the First World War was not just the result of lucky coincidence. He created his own opportunities. In 1917 he was finally called up for military service, but then opened up his own

Fantasy sketch for the Herrmann garden pavilion, Luckenwalde, 1920
Pen and ink

Fantasy sketch for a high-rise building, 1919

office in Berlin's Westend on the same day he returned to the city, 7 November 1918, in order to start work on his first commission: the Einstein Tower in Potsdam.

In early 1919 Mendelsohn held eight lectures, illustrated by episcope images in the salon held by Molly Philippson, a friend of his wife's, Luise. His comments culminated in the thesis that the new age demanded new architecture using a new building material, reinforced concrete. New forms would evolve from industrial architecture. Some of those present were so impressed that they soon entrusted Erich Mendelsohn with building commissions, among them Gustav Herrmann (Luckenwalde Hat Factory), Hans Lachmann-Mosse (Rudolf Mosse Publishing Company, Woga Complex) and also Walter Sternefeld.

In autumn 1919, Mendelsohn exhibited 42 drawings under the title *Architecture in Iron and Concrete* in Berlin's famous Galerie Cassirer. "The title sounded a little dry and uninspired, and of course no one had really heard of the architect. Only a few people wandered through the rooms, viewing sketches hung at eye level, relatively small sketches in an expanse of white, with the designs enlarged in a more dramatic manner up above. The strange thing was that from the first moment I felt myself caught up in the current, felt a rhythm leading me on, which I was unable to resist. The effect was so compelling that on the very same day I looked Dipl.-Ing. Erich Mendelsohn up in the telephone directory and called him. ... I visited him the next day in his studio near Reichskanzlerplatz, way up on the top floor with a view over the lush greenery of the Westend. An unpretentious, average-sized man in his early thirties approached me. The broad, clear lines of his face, showing no agitation, and his bright blue eyes behind severe, rimless glasses, were remarkable." Thus the description penned by the journalist Oskar Beyer in 1961, relating his first encounter with Mendelsohn, whose reputation he would greatly enhance.

The exhibition showed only a small portion of the architectural fantasies that Erich Mendelsohn had begun to develop in 1913, and on which he would base all his future work. Mendelsohn treasured these sketches for the rest of his life. In 1948 he told students in Los Angeles, "I believe that all creative artists reveal their individual importance in their first works. Later, this first outflow – which is bursting with ideas – provides a key to everything that is to come. Because if the first idea is profound enough, one lifetime will be too short to completely exploit it."

Mendelsohn took on every imaginable building task in the fields of industry and transportation. Important designs were created during his night watches on the Russian front to the west of Jakobstadt/Jekabpils (Latvia), where paper was at a premium and the sketches were consequently small. Some of the ideas from these "sketches from the Russian front" were later enlarged upon – for example the Einstein Tower or the Universum Cinema. His "musical sketches" were created while listening to the compositions after which they were often even named, such as "Bach Toccata in D major" or "Animato".

The exhibition of his sketches helped Mendelsohn establish a number of important contacts; in the following year, the Dutch architect Theodor Wijdeveld dedicated an entire issue of his influential journal *Wendingen* to Mendelsohn, he was invited to give a series of talks, became acquainted with the leading Dutch architects, which led him to a succinct description of his working method, derived from the contrast between the "visionary" Amsterdam School around Michel de Klerk and the "analytical" approach taken by the Rotterdam architects. "Oud is, in Gropius's words, functional. Amsterdam is dynamic. A union of both terms is imaginable, but nowhere to be seen in Holland at this point. The former requires a rational attitude – recognition through analysis. The latter requires an irrational one – recognition through vision. ... Function, of course, is the primary element, but function without a sensual component is just construction. Now, more than ever, I make a case for my programme of reconciliation. Both are necessary, both need to find their way to each other. ... The functional dynamic is the postulate."

Mendelsohn's designs were preceded by meticulous preparation. He began by visiting the building site. He spent hours sketching the surrounding landscape, the streets, the neighbouring buildings and the lines of sight, he noted the direction of the sun's rays and the wind. He studied the building requirements, the number and the size of the rooms, the client's wishes. Mendelsohn was also so successful because he showed an understanding of the client's position – which did not necessarily prevent heated discussions. But he would never have considered realizing an artistic idea contradictory to the client's requirements.

Once he had committed the basic conditions to memory, he relied on his intuition. Mendelsohn's designs were generally created at night, when he was working alone in his office or his bedroom – listening to music by Johann Sebastian Bach. Mendelsohn's birthday was on the same day as the composer's, and he felt a strong connection to Bach's music throughout his whole life. In June 1915, just after listening to Bach's Chaconne, he wrote, "This music does so much to turn everything into something larger, purifies our thoughts and suddenly shows forms that were desired as solutions. It is so great that it can create a synthesis out of the most confused matters." Ideas often came to him during classical concerts, and he would quickly sketch them out on the programme.

Mendelsohn sometimes experimented with different solutions, looking for the best one. But his greatest concern was almost always with the characteristic exterior view

Rudolf Mosse Printing and Publishing Company Building, Berlin, 1921–1923
The decisive idea for the corner came to Mendelsohn during a performance of Bach's Passion of St Mathew – he recorded it with just a few lines on the libretto.

from the perspective of the corner. "My sketches are data, fixing the contours of a sudden vision. In terms of their architectural nature, they appear immediately in their entirety and need to be treated as such. Their birth is essential, it contains the essential nucleus, which only becomes pleasantly human through development."

"I cherish the first sketch", he wrote in 1928 under the title "My Working Method". "Since as an experience, as a vision it condenses reality, plan and construction into an architectural organism. One idea, one creation. – Everything else is work, details of the layout, the construction, etc., but always fed by the experience, the experience always re-examined by the intellect. The work often leads to detours, i.e. rationale and calculation wage a pitched battle against intuition. But in the end the first sketch maintains its validity. ... Since the intellect builds, but intuition gives form."

Mendelsohn, who had never really learned the "craft" of the architect, entrusted all further work to his staff, whereby he monitored the "transformation of this sketch into a detailed building plan with painstaking care", as Julius Posener, who worked in his offices in Berlin and Jerusalem, reported. Mendelsohn always worked with models, which he used to work out the details of his buildings, before making new sketches, and then a final model out of clay and then, later, wood or plastic, which he presented to his client.

Posener later described Mendelsohn from the perspective of a young employee, saying, "I found him authoritarian. It was possible to engage in pleasant conversation with E.M. – after office hours. ... He aroused some personal antipathy on our part by drawing his pencils and making such an affair out of how productive we were, thereby playing one of his favourite roles. At the same time, we admired him. Ultimately we were also grateful, ... that had to do with his culture. He was one of the most charming people I have ever met – and at the same time one of the most unpleasant ones."

Mendelsohn found himself in between various fronts with his synthesis of analysis and vision, of functionality and dynamism. His architecture is Expressionist in the

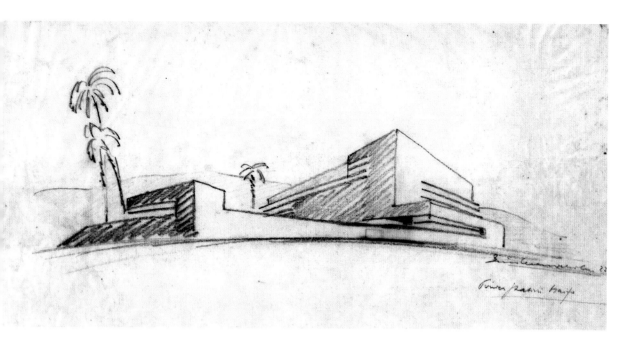

Sketches for an electric power plant in Haifa, 1923
Pencil on paper

sense that he realized his "visions", relied on his subconscious, his intuition. It is radically subjective, individual, poetic and anything but "scientifically" objective, such as was called for by the Bauhaus. At the same time, Mendelsohn's architecture "functions"; it is based on an analysis of the building task and not just fantasy architecture, as was the case with the Expressionist sketches by Sant'Elias, Finsterlin or the younger Bruno Taut. With this approach to architecture, Mendelsohn could not play a part in 'International Style'. Although he was respected, Mendelsohn did not belong to the self-proclaimed avant-garde. But that did not seem to bother him.

Early on, Mendelsohn established an international network. He enjoyed travelling. In 1923 he attempted to win a contract for a large project in Palestine, without any success. He travelled to the United States in 1924 and – as the first Western architect – to the Soviet Union in 1925 and 1926, he published the numerous photographs from these trips in a book along with a manifesto-like text. He found the experience in the United States both fascinating and sobering, "Land too young and uncertain, impulsive, exploitative, record delirium, unconsolidated, without traditions".

After the Inflation ended in 1923/24, Mendelsohn began to do a great deal of business. While most of his progressive colleagues had to live from public housing projects, he was able to devote his efforts to more lucrative private commissions. Success gives rise to envy, and in 1934 he wrote to Walter Gropius: "I know there are those who are against me, especially those fed by Giedion and Morton Shand. ... Everyone is free to adopt a friendly or an unfriendly attitude towards my work. But I revolt when people call me a mere businessman willing to do anything for a commission, as a means of belittling my achievements." Indeed, his arrogance kept him from making cheap compromises. When a client asked him to orient his design to an earlier building, Erich Mendelsohn answered: "Would you have asked Beethoven to write another seventh symphony when he was ready to write the ninth? You will get a Mendelsohn, and that is all that I can tell you."

House Am Rupenhorn, Berlin, 1928−1930
The music room was the largest one in the villa.
Music played a major role in Mendelsohn's life,
not only because Luise Mendelsohn was a cellist.

In 1930, Mendelsohn and his family moved into an impressive villa in the western part of Berlin – barely three years later he had to leave his native country. It was a farewell forever. Mendelsohn became a British, and then later an American citizen, changed his first name (1939) to "Eric", while his wife became "Louise". When he was invited to participate in an exhibition in Darmstadt in 1951, he replied: "As long as Germany does not have the courage or the insight to publicly erradicate the crimes against culture committed in its name, and with its silent approval, I cannot, as a Jew, contribute to the cultural importance of your land."

As Luise Mendelsohn later explained, "Perhaps it was just his uncompromising character, which, because he was so very German, caused him to adopt such an unforgiving attitude towards the political developments in his native country." Indeed, as late as September 1932 he had written from Thuringia about the "verdant dream of the late summer in the North, the mysterious magic that is called Germany and in which we are all caught up".

In the first months of his exile, in Amsterdam, Mendelsohn worked on plans for a "Mediterranean Academy" near Saint Tropez on the Côte d'Azur. While the Bauhaus brushed tradition aside, Mendelsohn, Wijdeveld and the French painter Amédée Ozenfant, the initiators of the project, intended to work towards modern development in various areas of culture: architecture, painting, theatre, music, film, dance, etc. on the basis of historical experience. Among the members of the advisory board for this fascinating project were Einstein, van de Velde, Berlage, Frank Lloyd Wright, Max Reinhardt, Strawinsky and Paul Valéry.

Presumably in order to meet financial backers, Mendelsohn travelled to London in summer 1933 and decided to stay there. For three years he maintained a joint office with the young architect Serge Chermayeff, but as of 1934 he began to shift the focus of his work more and more towards Jerusalem, where he established a second office. In 1939 he left London behind him, and then Palestine as well, when he relocated to the United States in 1941.

Asked in July 1933 why he did not go directly to Palestine (the official name of the country until 1948), he answered, "All of the attempts to work for our land have failed ... All those years I envisioned a Palestine built up by my own hand, its building industry brought into a cohesive form through my efforts, its intellectual structure put in order through my organizational talent, and then directed towards a goal. But Palestine did not call me."

In December 1934, when he was indeed in Jerusalem, he wrote, "In my innermost self I am determined to stay here. What the country needs most are creative people. ... We will live quietly for ourselves, for our work – for our people. There is no other, no greater task." The buildings he designed in England, in order to make a living during the first years of his exile, remained merely an intermezzo – albeit an important one for modern British architecture.

His ideas about building in "Eretz Israel" were not received with much enthusiasm. Young architects dominated the scene, among them many graduates of the Bauhaus who hoped to realize ideas in Palestine that they had developed in Central Europe. Mendelsohn, however, sought a synthesis between Western Modernism and local tradition, i.e. the experience of the indigenous Arab population. His goal was a combination of Orient and Occident, not the creation of another piece of Europe in Asia.

Anglo-Palestinian Bank, Jerusalem, 1936–1939
The headquarters of the largest bank in Palestine was the first high-rise building in Jerusalem. Mendelsohn's building combines modernity with understated solidity.

Characteristically, he established his office and his home in an old Arabic windmill in Jerusalem, not in the established Jewish city of Tel Aviv.

He formulated his basic thoughts in a 1940 publication entitled "Palästina und die Welt von morgen" (Palestine and the World of Tomorrow): "Palestine is not an unpopulated country. On the contrary, it is part of the Arab world. The problem that Jews in Palestine face is how to attain an equal footing with their neighbours, how to become a cell in a future Semitic federation of states to which they, by virtue of their race, their language and their character, belong. ... Palestine is the place where intellect and vision – matter and spirit – meet. Both Arabs and Jews should be equally interested in the agreement required for this connection. The fate of Palestine, its ability to become a part of the new world that will replace the old one, depends on solving this question."

Consequently, Mendelsohn had to devise a whole new architectural language. It is characterized by cubic shapes, closed walls, small windows and natural stone cladding. It did not fill him with pride when young architects in Tel Aviv began to build "Mendelsohn Houses"; instead he saw his vocabulary degraded to a mere "fashion". "There is simply too much imitation and too little individual experimentation. ... There is still so much to be done", was the conclusion he drew after visiting an architectural exhibition in Jerusalem in 1940.

In charge of large building projects in a nationalistically charged environment, he was subject to envy on the part of his younger colleagues without, as he had expected, being seen as a model, hence Mendelsohn must have felt completely out of place: "Thus, I float in air that will never belong to me. Uprooted for the rest of my life ... We only have ground to stand on, when we keep both feet on the ground. But it has been taken away from us."

In March 1941, the Mendelsohns left Palestine for the United States. 54 years old in the meantime, Erich Mendelsohn spent three months travelling all over the country by car, prepared an exhibition at the MoMA, held talks at various universities and outlined his vision of the post-war era for *Fortune* magazine. Initially the Mendelsohns lived with friends on a farm in Croton-on-Hudson, north of New York City. In autumn 1945 they moved to San Francisco, where Mendelsohn established an office with two younger partners, John Ekin Dinwiddie and Albert Henry Hill. He did not receive his architect's licence until 1946 and immediately a new career opened up to him – as the architect of large synagogues. Again his architectural vocabulary changed to suit the building task and the surroundings. But, finally, his buildings were to take on a model character again – the four synagogues he built in the United States became typological models in this country.

The distance between Mendelsohn's standpoint and the dictates of International Style becomes evident in the following lines, which he wrote after visiting Mies van der Rohe in Chicago in 1950: "He has found his formula and apparently intends to remain loyal to it up until the end. Block-like and academic, a canon of details, a rigid system of principles that will snuff out our emerging hope for human freedom swiftly and painlessly. ... He doesn't recognize that he is heading towards a dead end, one that leads nowhere." Even if Mies became the most influential figure in post-war architecture – it was Mendelsohn who was right in the end.

In spring 1953, Erich Mendelsohn was diagnosed with a tumour, half a year later he died in San Francisco on 15 September 1953 at the age of 66. Mendelsohn's ashes were strewn over the Pacific as he had stipulated. He was denied the opportunity to produce

Mendelsohn's residence in Jerusalem, 1935–1941
In Jerusalem, Mendelsohn lived and worked in an old Arab windmill in the Rehavia district, which was populated mainly by German immigrants. The flat was on the upper floor, his own studio was in the upper tower room.

Temple Emanu-El, Dallas, Texas, 1951
Sketch of ideas for the interior

a body of work in old age. But even having been able to work as an architect for as many years as he did, was never possible without worry. He was deferred from military service because of poor eyesight in 1914, and his left eye had to be removed in 1921 because of cancer. After that, he always lived in fear of losing the other eye. Almost all of his work was designed and built without binocular vision.

1918–1924 · Einstein Tower
Potsdam, Germany

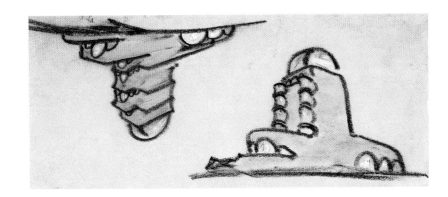

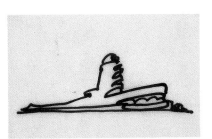

Three sketches

"This is how I imagine it", was how Erwin Finlay Freundlich began the letter he wrote to Deputy Sergeant Mendelsohn on 2 July 1918 explaining his clearly defined requirements for an observatory building in which he hoped to prove the validity of Einstein's Theory of Relativity. The ongoing discussion concerning the construction of an observatory between Mendelsohn and the astrophysicist, who worked in Potsdam, finally led to this "heavenly project" (Mendelsohn), which was to suddenly make the young architect world famous.

He completed the first sketches while still on the front, and was able to present his plans in Potsdam in June 1919. Due to resistance on the part of the city building authority, it was not possible to start construction until late summer 1920, based on the sixth revised plan. In August 1921 the building shell was finished, in January 1922 the laboratory was in operation, and the official dedication ceremony took place at the end of 1924.

However, in 1919 English experimental data had already proved the assumptions that were to be tested in Potsdam. Hence, the tower, for which a great number of donations had been collected, was quietly transformed into a monument, to Einstein, to astrophysics, to the importance of science in a vanquished German Reich. Mendelsohn created an unadorned, highly dynamic sculpture of a building that appears to have been formed out of some malleable material – the opposite of the process of building with concrete. And this leads us to the "myth" of the Einstein Tower. Because the building is by no means, as is often implied in the literature, made of concrete – a fact on which Mendelsohn chose never to comment. In 1920, there was a shortage of cement in Germany and it was very expensive, hence the building was made of brick; only a few parts were made of poured concrete.

Mendelsohn, a "beginner" in construction, succeeded in including a number of details despite the criticism from the city building office – but revenge followed swiftly. Dampness seeped into the walls from all sides; there were numerous cracks and rust spots. In 1927, the rough-grained, ochre-coloured stucco was replaced by a protective coat of opaque white paint. The windowsills and parapet around the dome were clad in

Opposite page:

Cross sections of the building from the period when construction was begun, September 1920

The orange sections were to be built of brick, the grey ones were to be poured concrete.

A view of the workroom with its Expressionist furniture, 1922

tin. Yet the Einstein Tower still required extensive renovation – something about which the public heard little. The Einstein Tower became famous as it appeared for just a short time in 1924, an image propagated by Mendelsohn and effectively emphasized in suggestive sketches. The tower became a prime example of a new, simultaneously functional and Expressionist architecture. It came to be seen as the ideal example of architectural Expressionism.

Mendelsohn was, however, strongly criticized by his colleagues. In 1923, Paul Westheim condemned its "monumentality ... lacking objective engineering perception, which is – despite a form of expression that appears to be modern – in essence similar to the Battle of the Nations Monument and the Bismarck on the Rhine. This tower near Potsdam is like a giant poster." And he charged Mendelsohn with the "grand self-confidence, peculiar to the genius and the dilettante".

View from the southeast

In 1999, the tower was restored to its original condition, extensively renovated and protected by state-of-the-art building technology. Still in use as an institute for gathering data on solar and nuclear physics, some of the interior details have been preserved and it is fascinating to see how carefully planned they are.

At the centre of the ensemble is a red wooden tower for the coelostat. Sunlight is reflected down into the cellar through it, where it is diverted at a 90° angle into a spectrograph room where it is split into its component parts and measured. In this room, constant temperatures were required, hence soil was piled up around it. Small additional workrooms are in the cellar and another one is situated on the ground floor, over the spectrograph room. Its semi-circular outer wall is cleverly perforated by windows that project at an angle. The room's effect is heightened by the contrast between the light walls and the greenish black paint on the reveal of the windows and the crystalline Expressionist furniture. The room above, used for sleeping, was in shades of blue; its original furniture has been lost.

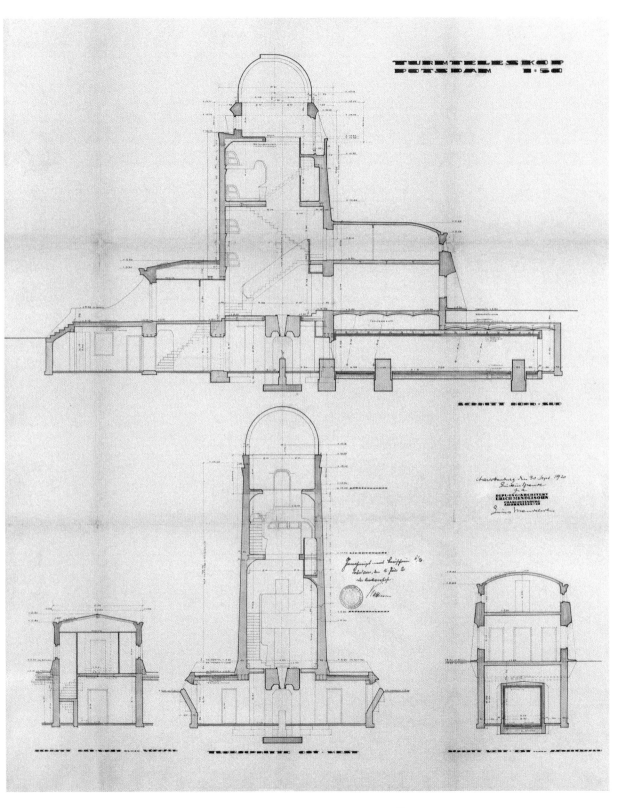

1921–1922 ▸ Double Villa on Karolingerplatz

Berlin, Germany

Above and opposite page above:
Views of the double villa, seen from Karolingerplatz and from Frankenallee
From the gate, paths lead left and right to the two separate entrances.

The names Dr. Kurt Heymann and Erich Mendelsohn appeared on the building permit application submitted in September 1921; a short time later, when the outer shell of the double villa was completed, Mendelsohn sold his half to a new owner. At the time Mendelsohn was living with his wife and daughter in three rented rooms in the nearby guest house "Westend". He obviously felt quite comfortable living in a situation where he was not encumbered by property.

To this day, few changes have been made to the double villa. Like most of Mendelsohn's buildings, it was developed from the outside, as can be seen in the surviving sketches. Here, on Karolingerplatz, a quiet, beautifully landscaped square, he chose not to emphasize the street corner, but instead opted for a staggered arrangement in three stages, leaving space for a small courtyard between the garden gate and the house. "The Karolinger corner is going to be rather amusing", he wrote in July 1922.

The floor plan shows two nearly perfect, interlocking squares. The two halves mirror each other along the central axis, i.e. a line drawn from the corner bisecting the angle formed by the two streets. The two rooms on this axis (per floor) belong to the one half of the house or the other, alternating from floor to floor, so each half has four

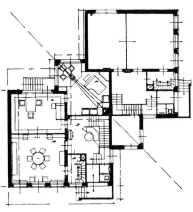

Floor plan

floors that are laid out differently. The utility rooms are located in the partially sub-merged basement. The living areas are on the ground floor, and the bedrooms are on the first floor. The smaller top floor, not visible from the street, is an attic and a sun terrace. The entrances are on the two long sides; the stairways leading to the doors are behind low walls that project from the otherwise smooth façade.

Like so many of Mendelsohn's buildings, this double villa seems "top heavy", a phenomenon on which Mendelsohn never commented, but which may have been intended to pique people's curiosity and make them walk around the building to examine it. The charm of this angular, unembellished building results from the unusual disposition of the building's mass and the imaginative nature of its façades: the corner windows are arranged in alternation, other small windows are grouped in bands of stucco. In addition, the division of the façades into lighter stucco areas below and dark, brick-clad areas above (in striped relief) are a reversal of the expected. Mendelsohn also designed cubic furniture for the living areas in one of the units.

1921–1923 ▸ Steinberg, Herrmann & Co. Hat Factory
Luckenwalde, Germany

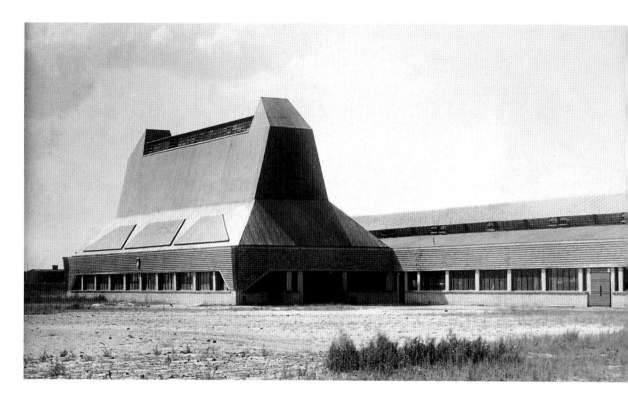

View from the southeast showing the dyeworks to the left and the boilerhouse to the right behind the production halls

In 1920, Mendelsohn built a group of small houses for Gustav Herrmann, conventional in form, but painted blue and yellow. A factory building similar to the Fagus Works designed by Gropius and Meyer had been erected in 1920 but burned down in 1925. After the two hat factories in Luckenwalde merged, Mendelsohn was commissioned to design a new factory complex on the outskirts of the city, in 1921: a symmetrical arrangement of four elongated, low-rise production buildings, flanked in the central axis by two buildings nearly twice as high, the dyeworks and the machine plant. The dyeworks building with its high, hat-like roof, through which the poisonous vapours set free during the dying process could be evacuated by natural ventilation, augmented by a mechanical system was a landmark until it was demolished by a new owner in 1935. On either side of the factory driveway, Mendelsohn built gatehouses with cantilevered roofs extending towards each other. Over the concrete foundations each of the buildings has a band of fenestration with a band of bricks over it, the brickwork is continued down to the concrete foundation at the corners. This made the complex appear to be uniquely dynamic despite its angular, crystalline lines. Mendelsohn also created an impression of lightness within the buildings: the reinforced concrete supports and beams supporting the saddle roofs with their glass riders become more slender towards the bottom and the middle of the building.

Left:
Inside one of the four halls

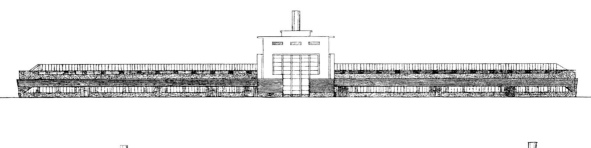

Mendelsohn submitted his plans to the Luckenwalde building authority, where a young Viennese architect had just begun working at his first job. His name was Richard Neutra. After seeing the drawings, he went to Berlin, introduced himself to Mendelsohn and was immediately hired. Mendelsohn entrusted Neutra with the details of the Rudolf Mosse Printing and Publishing Company Building and designing the surroundings of the Einstein Tower. He even considered making him an equal partner, although Neutra was five years younger, but ultimately decided against surrendering the power to make decisions alone. In 1923, Neutra left for the United States where he became an important architect in Los Angeles.

The innovative ventilation system in the dyeworks helped Mendelsohn to secure a very prestigious commission afterwards; in 1925, he was invited to work on a project in the Soviet Union – as the first architect from the West. His design for the Red Flag Textile Factory in Leningrad, including three dyeworks, was only partially realized; most of the plant still exists today, although in poor condition.

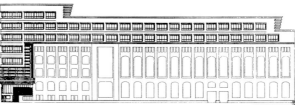

1921–1923 ▸ Rudolf Mosse Printing and Publishing Company Building
Berlin, Germany

The corner of the historicist sandstone building occupied by the Rudolf Mosse Printing and Publishing Company, one of the most influential in Germany, sustained considerable damage during the Spartacist Revolt of 1919. Consequently, Hans Lachmann-Mosse asked a number of architects to submit designs – all of which kept with the style of the old building. However, the publisher was looking for something else: he wanted something new, architecture that would cause a stir.

Erich Mendelsohn designed just that – he completely opened up the façades and integrated a cylindrical element with a strong horizontal emphasis into the building, which was not even 20 years old. It was made of different materials, iron, ceramic and smooth stucco, but he made no further changes to the original building. The entrance is emphasized by an extended canopy. Above it, wide bands of fenestration are layered one over the other, extending across the entire building on the two upper floors. The corner is emphasized by an additional storey. The stucco storeys appear to be even more dynamic as they fan out at the end. The result is a building with a breathtaking presence, particularly when viewed from the corner. "The dynamic motion of the new age suddenly emerges from the old façade, as if splitting it apart," a contemporary critic remarked.

With the Rudolf Mosse Printing and Publishing Company Building, Mendelsohn proved himself as an urban architect par excellence. He reaffirmed his affinity for the city, its traffic, its pace, its specific dynamics, its crowds and its bright lights. He saw the city as a complex structure, joined together at every intersection. Hence, for him the most important part of a building was the corner, which extends further into the rush of traffic, giving it direction. The building testifies to being part of its surroundings, and at the same takes over an active role because of its dynamics. In Mendelsohn's office the building was referred to as "the *Mauretania* steaming into Berlin's West Harbour".

Mendelsohn's role in redesigning the interior of the building is unknown. Publications only featured images of the main executive office redesigned by Mendelsohn's employee Richard Neutra. Erich Mendelsohn commissioned the sculptor Paul Rudolf Henning to model the ceramic elements for the façade.

After being damaged during the war, the building was reconstructed in a simpler manner, but in the 1990s it was fully restored. One of the two older parts of the building was rebuilt in a modern style, while Mendelsohn's addition was, for the most part, faithfully restored.

1923–1924 ▸ Villa Sternefeld
Berlin, Germany

Opposite page:
The attention of passers-by on Heerstrasse is
drawn to the entrance, which is recessed
mysteriously in shadows, by the subtle design
of the stairway leading up to it.

Right:
View from the northeast

Sketch of a version that was never realized
View from the southeast

The first single-family house built of reinforced concrete in Berlin was erected on a corner lot full of pine trees on the outskirts of the city. Its flat roof was also rare for Germany at that time. Among the house's striking features are its fundamentally cubic form, its top-heavy appearance, its austere horizontal lines and the way it seems to reach out into its surroundings. The exterior walls are covered with rough, sand-coloured stucco, the white woodframe windows fit smoothly into the outer skin of the house with the exception of the first upper storey where they are set into a recessed band of brick with pronounced cornices. The contours of the building are underlined by layers of brick on the cornices of the roof and the terrace.

This makes the Villa Sternefeld reminiscent of the prairie architecture created by Frank Lloyd Wright, while also exhibiting the influences from contemporary Dutch architecture. The interior is conventionally divided into individual rooms. The arrangement of the windows is determined by the exterior design, and not by interior functions; Mendelsohn later admitted to "having overemphasized formal aspects".

Inside, the ground floor was divided into an eastern half, which included the entrance and space for the Sternefelds' medical practice, and a western half with a living area that led out to a terrace. The kitchen and a utility room were located on the northern face of the building, in a one-storey extension. Its roof, which served as a terrace from the rooms on the first floor, projects far beyond the entrance cut into the building's volume. On the southern side there was a conservatory with another roof terrace above. The bedrooms were on the first floor. The floor above had no windows, its small utility rooms opened onto an enclosed courtyard that provided an opportunity to sunbathe in private.

In 1932, the top floor was transformed into a separate flat and windows were installed in the outer walls. In the 1970s, the outer appearance, at least on three sides, was restored.

1923–1929 ▸ C. A. Herpich Söhne Furriers
Berlin, Germany

The front of the building overlooking Leipziger Strasse by day (left) and by night (right) in 1929

Below:
Cross section of an illuminated cornice

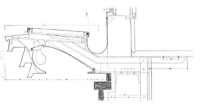

Before its destruction during World War II, the Herpich Furriers building was located on Leipziger Strasse, Berlin's main shopping street. A few hundred metres to the east, the glass front of the Tietz Department Store, designed by Bernhard Sehring (1899–1900), overlooked the same street; its curtain wall façade was the first of its kind in Germany, or perhaps the world. Alfred Messel's Wertheim Department Store (1896–1906) stood on the corner facing Leipziger Platz; its neo-gothic, vertical façades, glass-roofed inner courtyard and luxurious interior had become the prototype of German department store design – until Erich Mendelsohn arrived and blazed new paths in retail architecture.

Right:
View of the retail space in the main building

Below:
The scaffolding developed by Mendelsohn served as advertising space and attracted a great deal of attention.
After the second building phase, Mendelsohn's façade also encompassed the building on the left in this picture. The street lights provide a good sense of orientation when comparing this view with the one on page 32.

The Herpich project became Erich Mendelsohn's most bitterly contested building. City building authorities offered immense resistance – although the exact reasons are unknown. Mendelsohn succeeded in mobilizing famous colleagues to support him and even established a group called *Der Ring* to represent the interests of avant-garde architects. Construction was begun in 1925, but the complex was not completed until four years later.

Herpich Furriers occupied two older buildings with interiors that no longer satisfied the company's needs, and an exterior that was less than impressive. Erich Mendelsohn was charged with renovating the two buildings and expanding the complex to encompass an adjacent site, where the old building was to be demolished. He gave the complex, which was built in two phases, a uniform façade that made it look like it was built all at once. The building code in Berlin required the two new storeys to be set back to prevent them from casting shadows onto the street.

In designing the façade, Mendelsohn drew upon the lessons learned from two other department stores: Messel's Wertheim building, which had only small windows between its neo-gothic columns; and Sehring's Tietz building, in which the upper windows could be neither used effectively for display purposes, nor blocked by sales desks set up in front of them. Consequently, Mendelsohn avoided this sort of wasted space on the upper floors by designing walls tall enough for retail fittings to be positioned in front of them, but which left space between the wall and the ceiling for windows across the front, ensuring that the retail space was well illuminated (extensive

Leipziger Strasse branch, interior view

In 1927, Mendelsohn designed the interior of the Leipziger Strasse branch of C.A. Herpich. It featured tall shelving units and a band of illumination under the ceiling, an oval band of illumination in the ceiling and glass display cases in the retail area.

Below:

The entrance on Leipziger Strasse

artificial lighting was not yet a possibility). The ground floor was designed as a continuous display window. Here, at the latest, it became obvious that the façade was a non-supporting curtain wall. The starkly horizontal structure of the façade was framed by two bays on either side. Clad in Auer limestone and featuring bronze window frames, cornices and roofs on the bays, the façade attained a relief-like depth that contributed to its elegantly refined appearance. Concealed in the cornices under the windows, Erich Mendelsohn had tight rows of light bulbs installed that indirectly illuminated the façade after dark. Mendelsohn's illuminated cornices, his answer to the often thoughtlessly installed neon signs found on American department stores, were often emulated. The horizontal structure of the façade soon became the standard in German department store architecture.

Mendelsohn designed the retail space inside in a more formal, reserved style: illumination was provided by orbs of white milk glass, cubical cabinets against the walls, with smooth veneers and large mirrors, elegant leather armchairs and glass display cases set the tone. The only ornamentation was the carpeting in a style similar to that of Oriental rugs. During the construction period, Mendelsohn concealed the site with decorative scaffolding that also served as an unusual type of advertising. It was praised by the local merchants' association as an innovative breakthrough.

1925–1926 · Schocken Department Store

Nuremberg, Germany

View of the retail space

In 1924 the brothers Salman and Simon Schocken, from Zwickau, decided to expand their department store chain beyond the borders of Saxony. A modern company called for modern architecture and Salman Schocken chose Mendelsohn, whose work he had encountered at the Galerie Cassirer.

In November 1925, the company purchased property in a working-class Nuremberg neighbourhood, Steinbühl. To limit costs, the plan was to refurbish the existing factory building and to add a new building to it. Schocken targeted the mass market, the prices were low, and no luxury goods were sold. The customers were supposed to find the goods they were looking for quickly and easily without any seductive merchandizing, just like in a warehouse. Mendelsohn's design reflected this democratic business philosophy. Costly building materials were ruled out, the building was to be functional and serviceable. However, the façade had to attract customers, i.e. serve as advertising in itself.

In December, after only a month of planning, Erich Mendelsohn completed his preliminary work, and less than eleven months after the property had been purchased the store was opened. However, only the old factory building was renovated – difficulties with the building authorities had delayed the completion of the new building for so long that the project was finally abandoned. Instead, Mendelsohn designed a wooden structure in front of the old factory building, which was not recognizable as such at first glance.

The steel skeleton department store building was clad in brick with big shop windows on the ground floor. Continuous bands of windows on the three upper floors and the smooth wall area at the end gave the building a horizontal emphasis only slightly mitigated by the vertical columns that were left in place. The inner and outer appearance was simple and straightforward – like a warehouse. Mendelsohn had shelving for the merchandise installed under the windows. The stairways were located at the ends of the building – as could be seen from outside by the windows.

In his speech at the opening, Salman Schocken said, "The art of a true master can be recognized in the ability to select, to reduce, and to eliminate everything that is not essential, to limit the materials, to recognize the supporting pillars, to create what is needed with just a few essential lines." In the 1950s the building, which was extensively damaged during the Second World War, was remodelled to the point that Erich Mendelsohn's architecture is no longer recognizable.

Opposite page:
View after the opening in 1926
Because the building authorities had not yet granted a permit for the second building section, Mendelsohn extended a wooden portico in front of the main entrance all the way to the corner (left).

1926–1928 ▸ Schocken Department Store
Stuttgart, Germany

Opposite page:
Full view with the prominent stairway tower projecting outwards

Right:
The company used a sketch drawn by Mendelsohn for their guide to the department store.

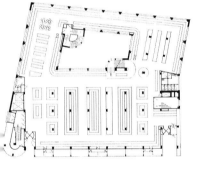

Floor plan

The Schocken Department Store in Stuttgart was the most important of Mendelsohn's retail architectural projects. It survived the Second World War, but was demolished in 1960, despite angry protest, only to be replaced by a typical example of the next generation of German department store architecture, a windowless cube designed by Egon Eiermann. The main argument of the new owner, the Horten department store chain, was that the open inner courtyard had no real function – the very element Mendelsohn had been forced to include by the building authorities in 1926. There were also plans at that point to widen the busy street in front of the department store, Eberhardstrasse – now it is a pedestrian mall.

Mendelsohn was confronted with a tremendously difficult building site. It was asymmetrical and had a steep slope, the differing widths of the surrounding streets allowed for different building heights. Using building volumes that varied in height between four and six storeys and had different façades, he succeeded in fashioning a building complex with a lively yet cohesive appearance. Erich Mendelsohn saw it as a "harmonious, contrapuntal architectural leitmotif" – the decisive idea came to him during a Bach concert. Two stairway towers serve as counterpoints to the broad expanse of the street frontage. The building's most characteristic feature was the fully glazed main stairway, completing the main façade on Eberhardstrasse. The ground floor was designed as a display window that subtly led passers-by to the main entrance next to the stairway. At night, the individual steps were indirectly illuminated from below. The administrative offices were located in the two upper storeys of the second tower. The steel skeleton construction was clad in very dark iron brick; the main façade also featured narrow stripes of costly Cannstatt travertine between the bands of brick and the deeply recessed windows (in reference to the location – Bad Cannstatt is a part

The viewing platform in the middle of the
retail space

Right:
View from the southeast
The second stairway tower forms a transition to
the lower sections of the building in the narrow
side streets.

Opposite page, above:
View from the southwest at night

Opposite page, below:
View into the glass main stairway

of the city of Stuttgart). Mendelsohn had to struggle to get the lettering on the façade, which was approx 7.5 feet tall and illuminated at night, accepted. He saw it as "part of the overall architecture. Which is why it does not simply float somewhere on the front wall, but is instead organically connected with the structure and the material of the display window unit. The letters are proportioned to correspond with the height of the window frames and the building as a whole."

The retail space inside was simply appointed, furnished mainly in wood. Air conditioning was not yet in use, so numerous windows provided ventilation. The grocery department was located in the basement where it was coolest.

The little guide to the store distributed to shoppers during the first weeks after it opened featured a coloured sketch of the building by Erich Mendelsohn that is just as ingenious as it is dynamic. Mendelsohn not only built three department stores for Schocken, which was the fifth-largest department store chain in Germany by 1930, he also developed an early form of branding, which encompassed the lettering of the logo, posters and advertising material.

1926–1927 · Bejach Country House
Berlin-Steinstücken, Germany

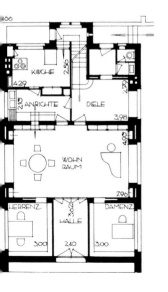

Erich Mendelsohn seems to have been pleased with the country house he designed for Dr. Curt Bejach – since he published numerous plans and photographs of it. The two-storey, flat-roofed house is set back from the street, spanning the width of the elongated site. The front lawn was for playing on, with a more private garden at the back, out of view.

A pergola along the right-hand side of the property leads up to the entrance to the house, on its narrower, northern side, next to the stairway, which projects from the centre, under the flat roof. Both the floor plan and elevation reveal unusual symmetries, beginning with the layout of the ground floor, the northern third of which is split in half, with the entrance, the toilet and the entrance hall facing the street, the kitchen and pantry the rear side. The middle third is made up of the big living room as wide as the house itself. The southern third is again divided into three parts: a small "hall" in the central axis leads out to the terrace, while the man's study and the woman's salon, both of which are accessed by the living room, are situated on either side. The upper floor is shorter in length by a third, because of the sun terrace to the south, and is divided into quarters. On the one side of the stairway and small central hallway, there is a maid's and a guest room, on the other a dressing room and a bathroom. The southern half of this floor is taken up by the master and the children's bedrooms, which have access to the terrace.

With pergolas and low terrace walls, the house extends into the garden in various directions and seems, on the whole, much larger than it really is. The external walls and the columns supporting the pergolas are decorated with attractive bands of stucco and brickwork. This feature, along with the flat cantilever roof, the wide windows on the ground floor, and the framing of the windows on the upper storey in an area of stucco, gives the house an extremely horizontal character. This country house, on the south-western periphery of Berlin, is well preserved.

1927–1928 · Petersdorff Department Store
Breslau, Germany (now Wrocław, Poland)

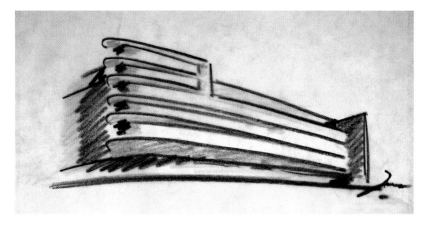

retail space, 1928

This well-preserved building in central Breslau, which is still used as a department store, has – unnoticed to most – an older structure behind its façade. Here again Mendelsohn brilliantly mastered a difficult building task: a garment store with a long tradition of purveying to the upper middle class occupied two old buildings on a street corner within view of the market square. The plan was to preserve one of the buildings and to replace the one on the corner. At the same time, the city decided to widen the side street, so that the building line was moved back considerably. Mendelsohn was expected to compensate for this loss of retail space in his design. Yet, the complex was still supposed to form an entity.

Mendelsohn installed a very unusual new façade on the old building overlooking the busier Ohlauer Strasse. It was made of smooth travertine with a row of tall, rectangular windows projecting out of it (as a rule, windows are embedded in the wall). He opened up the ground floor to install a continuous row of windows, which continued on around the corner of the building and into the side street, which was called Schuhbrücke. Next to the old building there was only space for a narrow new one, but Erich Mendelsohn extended its five upper floors out approx 6.5 feet over Ohlauer Strasse and Schuhbrücke (nearly 15 feet beyond the supporting steel girders). The continuous strips of travertine on the exterior wall, the heavy bronze cornices and the 165-foot-long, nearly floor-to-ceiling window fronts make this part of the building extremely dynamic – and the semi-circular bay windows are also an eye-catcher when viewed from the market square. At night, the bay windows were indirectly illuminated from above, across their entire width. A tall, narrow, illuminated sign displaying the name of the department store underlined the break with the historicist building next to it. The interior was designed by an architect from Breslau; seating for customers was installed in the bay windows. The entire construction period was less than half a year.

1927–1929 · Jewish Cemetery
Königsberg, Germany (now Kaliningrad, Russia)

The back of the main building, 1929

Mendelsohn did not practise his religion, but being a Jew was important to hi
throughout his life. His experience in Palestine in 1923 made such a great impressio
on him that later in the year he referred to himself in a letter as an "East Prussi
Oriental". Almost prophetically, he recognized the dangers of burgeoning Nation
Socialism quite early, and in the 1920s, when Germany was often in crisis and driftir
further to the right, he seems to have viewed the option of emigrating to Palestine
to the United States as an emergency solution. Since his student days, Mendelsoh
had acknowledged his commitment to Zionism, and he was also a great admirer
Martin Buber's writings.

Mendelsohn's very first building, designed in 1911 while he was still a student, w
a chapel for the Jewish cemetery in his native city of Allenstein. In 1925/26 he built
community centre in the East Prussian city of Tilsit, the Lodge of the Three Patriarch
and in 1930–1932 he built a very functional Jewish youth centre in Essen that went u
in flames in the *Reichskristallnacht* of 1938.

This fate was also shared by Mendelsohn's Jewish cemetery in Königsberg, one
two Jewish cemeteries in the East Prussian capital. This work occupies a very speci
position within Mendelsohn's œuvre, since it was the only one of his works in which I

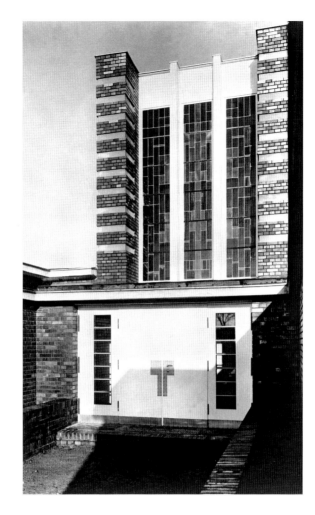

The entrance to the main building

The entrance hall is illuminated by glass windows designed by Carl Großberg.

had to master the task of landscape architecture. Outside of the cemetery gate there was a one-storey administration building with living quarters for the overseer, a gardener and a flower vendor. A central path led from the cemetery entrance through the symmetrically laid out graves of honour – outlined by hedges – to the main building, behind which the extensive lawns with the burial sites were to be found. Through a small "courtyard of the dead" one entered the funeral hall with a high central and two lower side naves. The elongated side naves were illuminated through a row of windows under cantilever roofs and had taharah rooms for the corpses of each sex. Mendelsohn designed this building, clad in black brick, in a simple, austere manner; the horizontal and vertical bands of stucco on the central nave represented the only ornamentation. The interior was "dark brown and bluish white and bronze" and featured two large glass windows at the front painted with geometric patterns.

1927–1931 ▸ Woga Complex and Universum Cinema

Berlin, Germany

This sketch from 1927 still shows elements that Mendelsohn eliminated from the building that was finally realized.

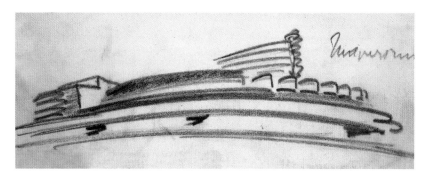

The residential buildings on Cicerostrasse

The Woga Project was the largest urban building project in Berlin during the Weimar Republic – the other big residential projects, like the Hufeisensiedlung, Onkel Toms Hütte or the Weiße Stadt, were built on the periphery. This complex, consisting of a big cinema, a cabaret, a row of shops, residential buildings and a hotel, was also the largest urban planning project that Erich Mendelsohn was ever able to realize. Designs for Haifa, in 1923, and for the White City in London, in 1935, never got off the drawing board. Mendelsohn had Hans Lachmann-Mosse, whose wife Felicia Mosse owned the *Wohnhausgrundstücksverwertungs-AG* (Woga), to thank for this major commission.

What is ingenious about Mendelsohn's design is the way he divided the project into four separate buildings, thus avoiding the common Berlin practice of building all around the edges of city blocks. The flat building for the Comedians' Cabaret and the Café Astor, now used for a pizzeria and a discotheque, was separated from the main building, with the cinema that is now a theatre, "Schaubühne am Lehniner Platz", by an access road (now a pedestrian zone). This public zone is closed off at the back by a six-storey, former apartment hotel set on piers. Behind it, on Cicerostrasse, there are long residential blocks with bands of brick (in alternation with cream coloured stucco), balconies that swing out and narrow, rounded entrances. Tennis courts were built in the middle of the block. The residential buildings on Albrecht-Achilles-Strasse, which runs parallel, were built by another architect, Jürgen Bachmann, whose most famous work was the Schöneberg Town Hall in Berlin.

The design of the cinema, the exterior of which was carefully reconstructed between 1976 and 1981 while the interior was completely revamped, could only be explained from the inside. As Mendelsohn said, "External structure developed on the basis of the disposition of the floor plan. A two-storey row of shops in front, entrance and box office, auditorium with a slightly sloping, turtle roof narrowing towards the back, shaft to raise the screen. Ventilation shaft with a slender display tower in front of it towards Kurfürstendamm." This ensemble allowed Mendelsohn to open up the otherwise dense construction along Kurfürstendamm, without creating a gap. He widened the street to form a plaza, inspiring pedestrians to walk past the rounded corners of the two buildings at the front of the row of shops. The connection to the

Opposite page:
The Universum Cinema in 1928

The second building section facing
Kurfürstendamm: the Comedians' Cabaret
(exterior and interior)

higher buildings around it was established through the ventilation tower and residential block at the end.

The Universum Cinema was often used by Europe's largest film production company, Ufa (Universum Film-AG), for premieres. The indirectly illuminated lobby was accessed through an entrance that extended far into the building. From there, stairways on either side led up to the balcony of the auditorium with a capacity of 1800. Behind the ticket office, a wrap-around corridor with adjacent cloakrooms surrounded the nearly oval auditorium on ground level. The elegant, but austerely functional cinema became a model for many film theatres in Germany and beyond.

With its bands of fenestration, staggered building segments and, not least of all, the slab-like wall that intersected the arc of the cinema's roof, the Woga Complex is very dynamic without overwhelming pedestrians the way the Rudolf Mosse Printing and Publishing Company Building did. The Kurfürstendamm ensemble attracts the attention of passers-by in a manner that is both confident and relaxed.

As with his other buildings, Mendelsohn held a speech at the dedication of the "Universum" in 1928. In it we read, "Cinema? Film, theatre of motion! Motion is life. Real life is authentic, simple and true. Hence, no posing, no sob stories. Neither in films, nor on screen, nor in architecture. Show what is within, what it means, what is sacrificed. ... Palace façades? Columned entrances for the worldly? Cathedral domes? For what! Turtle roof, protective arches of the slanted roof, slanted in the direction of the projection screen. ... No rococo palace for Buster Keaton, no wedding cake in plaster for Potemkin. But no need to fear! Not dry objectivity, not the claustrophobia of suicidal mental acrobats. Fantasy! Fantasy – but not bedlam – dominated by space, colour and light. ..."

**The Universum Cinema, view of the lobby
and the auditorium**
The interior was completely redesigned when
the building was converted into a theatre
(Schaubühne am Lehniner Platz).

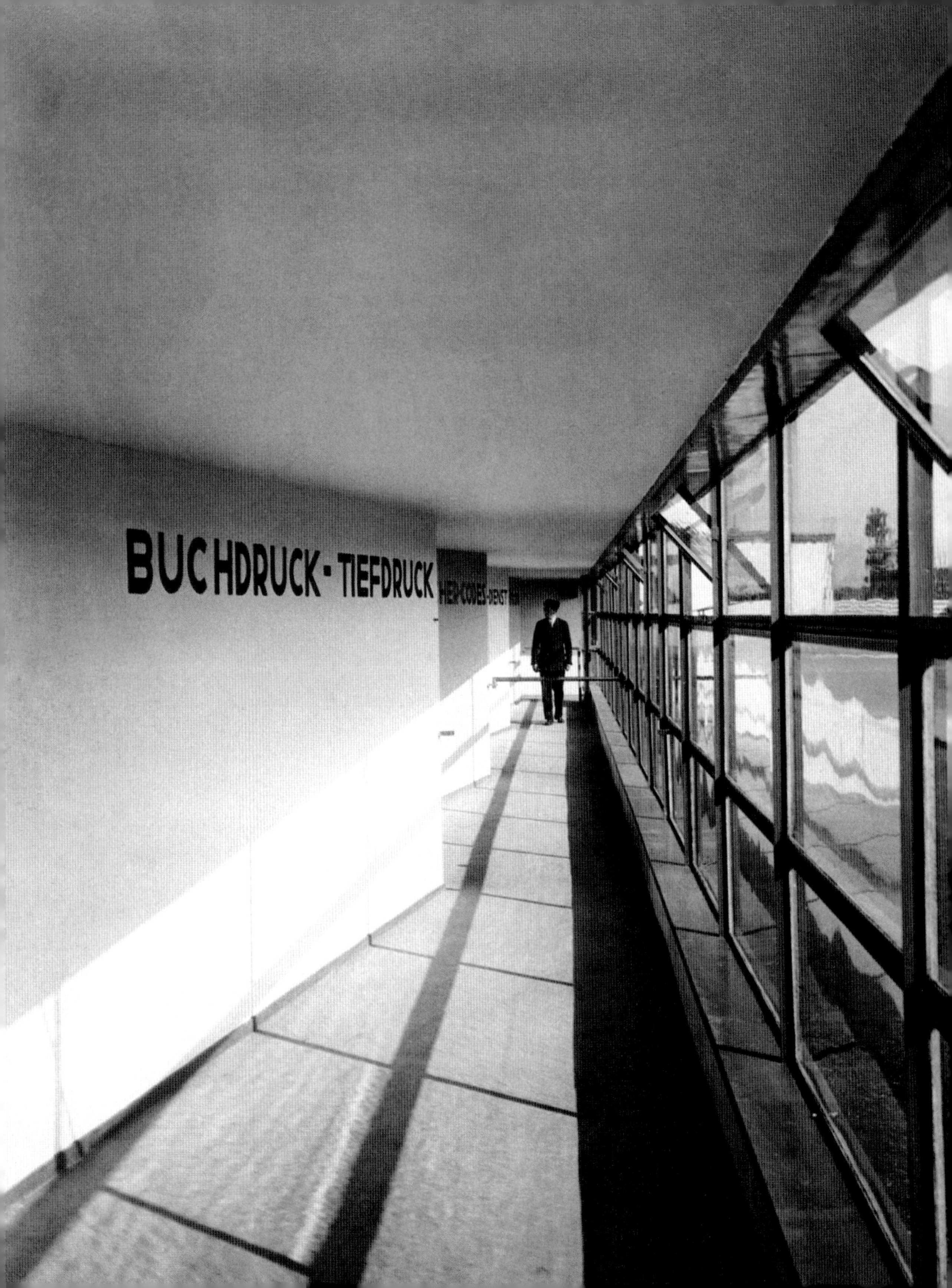
BUCHDRUCK - TIEFDRUCK

1928 ▸ Rudolf Mosse Pavilion
Cologne, Germany

On the upper floor, which projected further forward, radio was presented as the new medium.

The "Pressa", an international press exhibition staged at the exhibition grounds in Cologne from May to October of 1928, was one of the largest trade shows of the 1920s. It was not only the first extensive presentation of the achievements of the international press, but – because of the far-reaching radio, newspaper and magazine reports – it also became a major cultural exhibition. Numerous publishers and printing houses had exhibition pavilions built by famous architects. The Soviet pavilion, designed by the Constructivist El Lissitzky, with whom Mendelsohn had maintained friendly contact since his first visit to the Soviet Union (1925), attracted a great deal of attention.

Mendelsohn's pavilion for the Rudolf Mosse Printing and Publishing Company Building was also greatly admired. The pavilion with its light, iron frame and extensive glazing was disassembled at the end of the exhibition.

On the ground floor the publishing company presented its various products, while on the upper floor the latest devices for radio and news transmission were exhibited and demonstrated. Important breaking news was broadcast over a loudspeaker on the roof. The tall broadcasting mast displaying the illuminated "Rudolf Mosse" logo was, therefore, not only a symbolic eye-catcher, it also served a practical purpose.

Opposite page:
Interior view
From the entrance at the front, visitors were led down the longer sides of the pavilion. The individual exhibition rooms were located behind the diagonal partitions.

1928–1930 · Schocken Department Store
Chemnitz, Germany

Opposite page:
In this view from the side, one can easily see how the middle part of the façade projects forward.

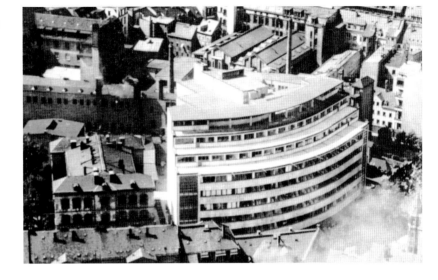

An aerial view from 1930 illustrates how innovative Mendelsohn's new architecture was.

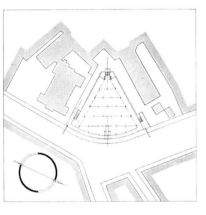

Site plan

The last and largest of Mendelsohn's department stores was relatively simple, both inside and outside. In the floor plans that he published, the building is laid out as a perfectly symmetrical isosceles triangle. The front is semi-circular, emulating the curve of the street. There are stairways, lifts and escalators in each of the three corners; the interior space is structured by reinforced concrete supports arranged on a centre-to-centre grid of nearly twenty feet. Objections on the part of the neighbours prevented this ideal plan from being realized, yet the slightly skewed floor plan is barely notice-able inside.

The symmetry of the street front can be recognized quite easily on the ground floor. It is divided into thirteen axes, with three large display windows spanned between each of the four entrances. The two external axes are occupied by the stairways, in between which the first five floors protrude out 3.2 feet across the full width of over 180 feet. Three further floors are stepped inward. With the exception of the stairways, which have small individual windows, the entire façade is arranged horizontally by alternating bands of fenestration and solid wall areas. Inside, permanent shelving for the mer-chandise was installed behind the outer walls clad in light coloured Au limestone.

Originally the wooden window frames were filled with clear glass so that during the day the row of reinforced concrete columns, 11.5 feet behind the façade, was visible from outside. Today, it is only possible to recognize the façade's structure and thin skin at night, when the lights are on inside. Mendelsohn underlined the fact that the façade of the bay was not a supporting wall, by installing a narrow band of windows between the big display windows and the bay.

1928–1930 ‣ Mendelsohn House
Berlin, Germany

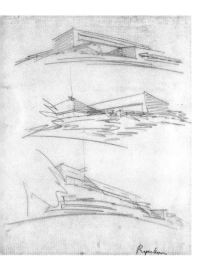

The sketch at the top shows the house from the street, the two below show the house from the garden.

Opposite page:
The way to the entrance through the front garden

"In this age of architectural materialism, it is revolutionary to say that a family consists of more than just people who sleep, wash themselves and eat, that it consists of intellectual and spiritual beings! Hence, the decor – I deliberately use the word – of their surroundings must be uplifting. It must be a source of positive inspiration, spaciousness and beauty. I wish everyone could have this kind of house." Thus the praise expressed by the French painter Amédée Ozenfant, culminating in the characterization: "a house for the Goethe of 1930", which not only Mendelsohn's critics found exaggerated. Instead of quietly enjoying his new home, Mendelsohn published a richly illustrated, trilingual book on it entitled *New House – New World* in 1932, which included a foreword by Ozenfant. It almost seems as if he built his house just to show it to the (architectural) world.

Mendelsohn once sketched a private house for his fiancée before their marriage in 1915: a three-storey villa for a family of five, plus personnel, centred around a music room and an art gallery. However, since 1919 the Mendelsohns had been living in three rented rooms in a guest house in the Westend. Independence was important to Erich Mendelsohn. "Everything depends on being mobile and unencumbered. Anyone who limits his mobility becomes rusty", he once wrote in a letter.

Nevertheless, Mendelsohn began the search for a suitable building site in 1926 – perhaps more out of consideration for his wife. In 1928, he chose a long, narrow site on a cul-de-sac called Am Rupenhorn on the outskirts of Berlin's Westend. The property had over 43,000 square feet and was situated on a high ridge overlooking the Havel, to which it had access, at the point were the river becomes as wide as a lake. They had a housewarming in the summer of 1930. Mendelsohn seems to have felt uneasy about it, in late 1928 he wrote to his wife, "Millions are calling for a war that will ultimately devour them as first victims. And what are we doing? ... Building a house ... We forfeit our most valuable asset, our quiet contemplation, our productive simplicity – for whom? Out of habit, out of lethargy, out of a tendency to swim with the current, for the sake of owning something, for the sake of pleasure or because we can afford it! We like to disguise these vanities as a desire for beauty and a need to strive for some ideal – but reality drains us and narrows our spirits."

This brick house was built with clean lines accented by white stucco. Laid out in a two-storey, L-form, it is an ideal site for quiet repose in the midst of nature. A high wall facing the street shields the property from view. From the entrance, a driveway leads to the garage, while an 82-foot pathway of paving stones leads straight to the narrow entrance. The front of the building is a little forbidding; there are no windows on the ground floor and the only opening in the façade is the band of windows just under the flat roof. The entrance is in a small, one-storey section, which also contains the kitchen. A corridor then leads into a "hall" with a seating area and a bay-like dining room to the right. The largest room in the house – the music room – is located to the left, accessed through an open doorway. The big window in the hall could be retracted into the floor by pressing a button. But in the music room there was no intention of creating

The music room with a copper relief by Ewald Mataré

Mendelsohn's study on the first floor of the northern wing
The view from the window extends to the Havel down below.

Floor plan

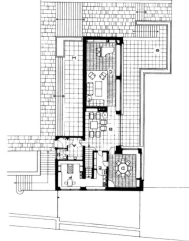

a seamless transition between indoors and outdoors; a window parapet with radiators formed a clear barrier, which was further emphasized by massive wall columns. The study, the bedroom, the children's room and the guest room on the upper floor are all oriented towards the west, i.e. the Havel. "The floor with the bedrooms is like a small hotel. Minimal scale. To each his own, each room with a bath, telephone and oriented to individual needs." (Mendelsohn)

On the basement level, there were not only utility rooms, but also a gym, under the terrace. Mendelsohn had all sorts of devices intended to make everyday life more comfortable, installed in the walls. Ozenfant: "Although current fashion dictates that we display our organs openly, we must recognize that a house is not a military inspection ... not a museum of mechanical development." Mendelsohn also designed

The furniture, individual pieces were made by the silversmith Emil Lettré and by the painter Amédée Ozenfant.

The Mendelsohns often entertained illustrious guests like André Gide, Salman Schocken, Theodor Wolff, Chaim Waizmann and Albert Einstein, who usually came by sailing boat across the Havel. The annual highlight was Mendelsohn's – and Johann Sebastian Bach's – birthday, which was celebrated with a house concert, in which Einstein played the violin. It is difficult to say how hard the Mendelsohns found leaving the house forever in 1933. We do know that only a year after moving in, Mendelsohn wrote to his wife saying that he found "the settled existence" in the new house restricting and oppressive".

In a view from the west, the window of the gym can be seen under the terrace.

1928–1930 ▸ German Metal Workers' Federation Building

Berlin, Germany ▸ with Rudolf W. Reichel

View from the southwest

After 1928 Mendelsohn received fewer commissions, parallel to the general economic situation. Since his office was too big to operate at capacity with just one or two projects, he took part in more competitions. He won a number of first prizes, but the only commission to result from one up to 1933 was from the metal workers' union, the *Deutscher Metallarbeiterverband* (DMV). Still used by the IG Metall, the successor to the DMV, the building is well preserved. The union asked five architects to submit designs in 1928. The two designs favoured by union leaders were by Mendelsohn and the Berlin architect Rudolf W. Reichel.

Since they were similar, both architects were engaged to develop the project together, with the details worked out by Mendelsohn's office. The building that was

View into a corridor in the side wing
The supporting columns are located in the wall to
the offices.

ultimately realized reveals only his handwriting; Reichel had not built anything remarkable up to that point, and he did not do so afterwards either.

Mendelsohn's original plan was for a large complex where the metal workers'
building would be connected to a similar long building running parallel to it on the
other side of a street that was being planned to divert traffic, Entlastungsstrasse. They
were to be connected by a four-storey bridge spanning the street. This second building
was to be used for the editorial offices and printing plant of the social democratic
newspaper *Vorwärts*. But the project was cancelled.

Thirty-three sketches drawn by Mendelsohn on a single sheet in January 1929 still
exist. In them he was seeking the best solution for the corner. Notably, he sketched a
number of alternatives for the same corner – this was the only task to resolve, the rest
of the building would (as was always the case with Mendelsohn) be developed from
there.

The building site was a perfect triangle; the room requirements foresaw impressive
offices for the board, administrative offices, space for the printing press and retail
space to be rented out. Mendelsohn designed a building arranged symmetrically along
its axis. The offices were located in two five-storey wings with space for retail shops and
a bookbindery on the ground floor. Between these two wings he spanned a two-storey
printing plant, at the back, and a six-storey main building in front where the site

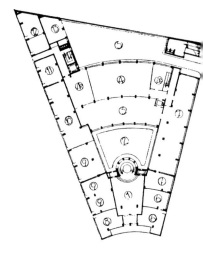

Floor plan

View of the stairway tower from the courtyard with the printing plant in front

arrowed. This building was slightly concave, leaving space for a small plaza in front, nd contained rooms for official functions and the offices of the union leadership. The op floor, which had much higher ceilings, featured an assembly hall with a big glass ay and a flagpole outside (like a standard bearer leading a demonstration). The main uilding is clad in shell limestone and has sliding windows with wide, rectangular ronze frames on the front while displaying the emblem of the union on either flank. he ground floor is fully glazed – since it is a steel skeleton construction with curtain alls. At the back of the main building an impressive stairway – forming a circle in plan - winds its way up in an elegant spiral. It is illuminated during the day by the light that omes in through the exterior skin of glass, and at night by a lighting element made of lass balls and fluorescent lights suspended from the ceiling.

The two wings of the building are finished in white stucco, the individual, wooden-rame office windows are along continuous sills. All the offices face the street. The orridors, stairways, lifts, and even the rooms of the printing plant that face the ourtyard receive light through continuous bands of fenestration – the supporting olumns are concealed within the walls between the offices and the corridor. As a esult, the view from the courtyard is unusually dynamic.

63

1931–1932 ▸ Columbus House
Berlin, Germany

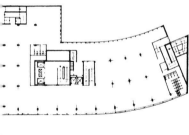

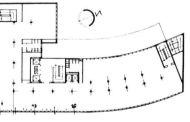

It is now common for office buildings to be designed so that the internal layout remains flexible, but the first large office building to be relatively free of internal supports was probably Erich Mendelsohn's Columbus House. Partially restored after damage sustained during the war, the steel skeleton building went up in flames during the revolt in East Berlin on 17 June 1953, and was demolished in 1957.

Martin Wagner became the Berlin Building Commissioner in 1926 intending to make the city's two main traffic hubs, the Alexanderplatz and the two neighbouring squares Leipziger Platz and Potsdamer Platz, into modern "world-class centres". The project was developed on the basis of a prognosis concerning the expected volume of traffic in the next twenty-five years. After that, the buildings would have fully depreciated and could have been replaced. Mendelsohn developed a number of alternatives for Leipziger/Potsdamer Platz, and entered into negotiations with the Berlin branch of the Paris department store chain Galéries Lafayette in mid-1928. At the end of the year, the old buildings were all torn down, and in January 1929 Mendelsohn hired Ernst Sagebiel as a construction site manager, the man who would later build the *Reichsluftfahrtministerium* (Reich Air Ministry) and Tempelhof Airport.

In February the project was suddenly interrupted – Building Commissioner Wagner had reservations because of the additional traffic that a highrise would cause in this overly congested area. Mendelsohn put a fence up around the building site, which could be rented as advertising space and also provided room for shops and the site manager's office. After months of stalemate, the partners in Paris withdrew from the project, and building did not resume until spring 1931 – now for a multifunctional

building with restaurants, shops and offices, but with three fewer storeys. After a construction period of only eleven months, one of the largest office buildings in Germany, with a volume of over 1,900,000 cubic feet, was ready for occupation – a major logistical achievement.

Commenting on his own design, Mendelsohn wrote, "In accordance with the actual task, to erect a building as part of a wall framing a public square, all emphasis on the corners has been avoided. Only the form of the roof and the continuation of the bands of fenestration indicate a clear orientation towards Potsdamer Platz. ... The layout of every floor has been reduced to the simplest formula. The overriding idea in distributing the space is to ensure that every imaginable use is possible in the future, so that any necessary changes will not require extensive reconstruction work."

Mendelsohn was confronted with a considerable problem: large plate glass windows were desired for the two lower floors, while the other eight storeys were to remain as flexible as possible. Hence, the structural supports could not be part of the façade below, and not in the middle of the floor space above. To provide an elegant façade free of structural supports at street level, Mendelsohn designed a steel skeleton structure for the upper floors with supports that were only 6.3 inches wide and a façade in segments of only 4.26 feet. Behind this grid, an area measuring 22 feet by 295 feet could be used flexibly. (A double row of columns at the centre of the building was

One of the completely variable office levels, flooded with light

integrated into the corridor walls.) The weight of the façade was transferred inward on the first floor via ceiling beams onto columns that were themselves less than 12 inches wide. Half of the steel used for the building was in the first two storeys.

The cantilever roof over the roof terrace, which was part of a restaurant, was also spectacular. Across the full length of 295 feet, the roof projected out over 21 feet without any supports. Skylights were installed in half of it, with heating coils to keep them free of snow in the winter. The street fronts were clad in limestone, and the letters of the neon signs were attached to tracks between the bands of windows, so that they could be changed easily. The Columbus House was the first high-rise office building in Germany with air conditioning. Water was drawn from the property's 105-foot well, filtered a number of times, and then fed into the circulation system. Two of the three building cores, each with a stairway, a lift, toilets and a paternoster, were located at the ends of the building, and one at the centre. On 1 October 1932, Mendelsohn relocated his Westend office to the Columbus House, half a year later he left Germany forever.

1933–1935 › De La Warr Pavilion
Bexhill-on-Sea, Great Britain › with Serge Chermayeff

The southern stairway

Henry-Russell Hitchcock, the curator of the 1937 exhibition on modern English architecture at the Museum of Modern Art (MoMA) in New York, called the De La Warr Pavilion "probably the most notable and successful modern building in England". Mendelsohn came to play a short, but important role in the history of modern architecture in England.

After emigrating from Germany, Mendelsohn spent the first months with his old friend and colleague Hendrik Wijdeveld in Amsterdam. In summer 1933 he went to London and decided to stay there – in order to establish himself as an architect. Mendelsohn, who had held a number of lectures in England a few years earlier, was welcomed by his colleagues. He even applied for British citizenship – a momentous step, since it meant that he had to forfeit all claim to his property in Germany – but, as a foreigner, he was not allowed to open an office on his own. Hence, in the autumn he bought a 55% share in an office established by a 33-year-old architect of Russian origin, Serge Chermayeff, who he had known since 1930. Chermayeff had very good contacts and had acquired quite a reputation as an interior designer. However, he had very little experience as an architect, and he greatly admired Mendelsohn. It was an ideal partnership that was to last for three years. Chermayeff was responsible for negotiating with clients, for the logistics and the interior design. Mendelsohn made all of the architectural decisions. Due to the conservative attitude of most of the potential British clients, Mendelsohn was only able to build three projects in Great Britain.

Shortly after establishing their joint office, Mendelsohn and Chermayeff won the competition to build the De La Warr Pavilion in Bexhill-on-Sea, a small resort town on the South Coast of England. Mendelsohn could hardly have dreamt of a better start than triumphing over 230 other architectural offices in a public competition. The building not only became a model for a number of English recreational and resort centres, it also became one of the most important reference works in modern British architecture. The original plan of a recreational complex was abandoned for reasons of cost, the only part realized was the pavilion named after the mayor, Lord De La Warr.

The site was located between the beach, to the south, and the main road, to the north. At the centre of the rectangular ensemble lies the entrance hall with the stairways at both ends. To the right of the hall, after entering from the north, there is a large auditorium, a theatre, which looks like an enclosed, white stucco block from the outside. To the left of the hall lies a narrower, two-storey tract with a bar, restaurant, cafeteria, dance floor and reading room. Seen from the sun terrace, which faces south, the building seems open and welcoming with its numerous windows. Seen from the north, where the kitchen and storage rooms are located on the ground floor, with a reading and other rooms on the floor above, the building seems cool and austere with its bands of ribbon windows high up on the walls. The most notable external feature is the southern stairway, the prestigious nature of which is also reminiscent of the one in the Berlin metal workers' building. The stairway winds its way up around a hollow newel in which a lighting element is hung. The stairway is enclosed in a glass cylinder framed by a supporting white metal structure. Each of the three floors is marked on the outside of the stairway by a wide inviting balcony. It ultimately leads to the upper foyer of the auditorium.

The interior, which is flooded with light through big windows facing south, is sparingly furnished and seems quite spacious – the furniture designed by Chermayeff and Mendelsohn creates an impression of refined luxury. As a steel skeleton construction, the building was also very innovative for Great Britain in terms of building technology.

View of the ocean side from the southwest

Above left:
The reading room on the first floor with furnishings designed, in part, by Mendelsohn.

Above right:
The stairway projected from the northern façade just beyond the main entrance.

The auditorium

1934–1936 › Weizmann House
Rehovoth, Palestine (now Israel)

The chemist Chaim Weizmann became the president of the Zionist movement in 1935 and the first president of the state of Israel in 1948. His villa in Rehovoth, south of Tel Aviv, is now a national monument.

Mendelsohn created a house that was adapted to the heat of the Mediterranean climate. Hence, it differed radically from his earlier buildings. The villa, visible from a great distance, is located on a hill and has a static and forbidding appearance due to its few windows and white stucco. Interestingly, Mendelsohn got visitors to the house moving by having them climb the hill on a path that led all the way around the building. The U-shaped building is perfectly symmetrical in an east-west direction, oriented towards the cool sea breezes. The entrance to the house is on the northern side, so that the symmetry is not immediately obvious upon entering. Attached to the two-storey volume in the middle, the central axis of which is augmented by a third storey, there are two single-storey wings, the open ends of which are enclosed by screens shielding the full-length roof terrace. The living areas have access to the inner courtyard through glass doors. Here the swimming pool is protected from the sun by cantilevered roofs.

The entrance hall and the dining room are located on the ground floor of the middle section, the living room, the study and the library are in the wings. The bed-

View from the garden in the west
Beneath the characteristic stairway tower, there
was a swimming pool in the shaded courtyard.

Below:
Interior view of the stairway tower

rooms and guest rooms are located upstairs. The most striking element in the house
is the stairway tower, which projects in a semi-circle into the inner courtyard – where it
is echoed by a semi-circular bay window across from it to the east. The impressive
stairway underlines the house's function as the residence of a statesman; it enables the
owner of the house to make a grand entrance – descending from the private rooms
into the entrance hall.

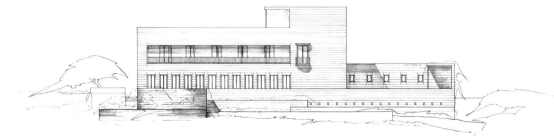

1934–1936 ▸ Schocken House and Library
Jerusalem, Palestine (now Israel)

Opposite page:
The library seen from the street
The only decorative element on the austere
southwestern façade is the glass bay.

Opposite page below:
The southern side in elevation (with the
protruding, semi-circular terrace on the left)

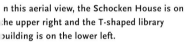

In this aerial view, the Schocken House is on
the upper right and the T-shaped library
building is on the lower left.

Mendelsohn had just arrived in Jerusalem when Salman Schocken commissioned him
to build a residence and a library. One of the two directors of the Zwickau department
store chain, Salman Schocken was a passionate book collector. After his older brother
Simon had been killed in an automobile accident (1929), he moved to Berlin and
founded the Schocken Publishing Company, and, in 1934, he emigrated to Palestine
with his wife. Amazingly, he was able to take his library comprising 60,000 volumes –
including numerous manuscripts and first editions – with him to Jerusalem. In 1935
Schocken bought the liberal newspaper *Ha'aretz*, of which he then became the editor.
In 1940 he moved to New York and in 1959 he died in Switzerland, at the age of 82.

The relationship between Mendelsohn and his most important client was one of
mutual respect. In Schocken's speech on the occasion of Mendelsohn's fiftieth birthday (1937), he asked, "How many people do you meet in the course of your lifetime,
where you think this is someone who is completely up to the demands placed upon
him, who lives for what he does, takes it seriously and is willing to pay a high price for
it? ... The experience of having highly original personalities is primarily one that in-
volves fighting. And I don't know anyone with whom I have fought as much as with
Erich Mendelsohn."

The construction of the villa and the library in Rehavia, an area where many German emigrants had already built villas, seems to have involved no major battles. "The
house is going to be beautiful, a kind of primary design inspiration. It is not at all like
Weizmann's." (Mendelsohn in December 1934) This was, above all, related to the very
different environment. The Weizmann House had to withstand the hot sea climate up
on a hill, while the Schocken House was located in the city of Jerusalem – albeit on a

The lecture and reading room on the upper floor of the library

From the left, light poured in through the bay window.

large, sloping site – where the climate is cooler. In addition, Schocken was not seeking public recognition. Consequently, the house made no attempt at being impressive.

It is an elongated, asymmetrical building with a staggered façade clad in natural golden yellow Jerusalem stone. Mendelsohn employed a method that was common in Jerusalem at that time: two walls were built up close to each other, then the space in between them was filled with concrete, and neuralgic points were reinforced with iron girders. The house opened onto the long terrace with numerous glass doors and, on the first floor, there was a wide, recessed balcony overlooking the southern garden. The only openings in the northern and front sides were a few small windows and a shady recessed balcony. On the ground floor the rooms were spacious: a music room, a living room, a dining room and Schocken's study, with the private rooms on the upper floor. The utility rooms were out in a small wing to the north. The model was obviously the Mendelsohn House (Am Rupenhorn), which the Schockens had greatly admired.

From the sweeping western area of the garden terrace there is a view of the library that Schocken wanted to make available to the public as a research institute – hence it was built on a separate lot. Mendelsohn wrote to his wife: "The building site makes no sense, but the plan has humour and Palladio." The two-storey, flat-roofed building is laid out in an irregular T- form, the entrance is to the right of the centre of the façade, the building segment behind it, which reaches far into the building, is organized along

The northern side of the Schocken House

one hip, i.e. the small study and reading rooms are all located on one side of the corridor. All this contradicts the symmetric ideal of the Italian Renaissance architect Palladio. Yet the library, which is clad in Jerusalem stone like the villa, displays a classic, almost archaic dignity and simplicity.

Notable is the semi-circular glass bay that projects from the southern façade. It provides light for the big reading room/lecture hall in which Mendelsohn installed floor-to-ceiling bookcases, all the way around, made from costly, light-coloured lemon-wood. He divided the northern wall into bookcases enclosed in glass, above which windows under the ceiling let in additional light. The three-storey book depository is located in the western part of the building and can be recognized from outside by a row of tiny windows. Today, there is a theological research institute in the library. In 2003, the demolition of the villa, which was used by the Academy of Music for many years, was prevented. To this day, however, Erich Mendelsohn's reputation in Israel still suffers from the fact that he left the country after only a few years.

1934–1939·Hadassah University Hospital
Jerusalem, Palestine (now Israel)

Opposite page:
View of the entrance, crowned by three
domes, from the hospital courtyard

The view from the balcony of the Chapel for
the Dead extends out into the desert.

Mendelsohn began working on a master plan for the Hebrew University of Jerusalem
on Mount Scopus, *Har Hazofim* in Hebrew, in 1934. It was a prestige project supported
especially by Schocken and Weizmann and planned for one of the most beautiful building sites in the city, replete with a view of the old city, to one side, and of the Dead Sea,
to the other. Mendelsohn's plans were submitted as Palestine's entry to the Paris
World Fair in 1937, but because of continuing disagreements between the university,
the British Mandate Government and American backers, only a few parts were ever
realized. One of them was by far the largest building Mendelsohn built in Palestine, the
Hadassah University Hospital, which was begun in 1936 and completed in 1939 after a
series of strikes. Closed from 1948 until 1967, it is now – greatly expanded – the largest
and most important hospital in Israel.

The western side of the nursing school was connected to the hospital by a covered passageway before the expansion of the complex.

Below:
View of the nursing school's veranda

Three building segments were completed according to Mendelsohn's plans: the hospital itself consists of two parallel buildings, which are three to four storeys high and connected by two middle segments. A 263-foot-long, covered promenade leads to the nursing school, a simple elongated rectangle with characteristically rounded balconies.

Mendelsohn's first model for the hospital was a dynamic design in which two of the three parallel wings were to be connected to each other in a big sweep. The building that was then erected is very static by comparison; only the sweeping terraces and the "Chapel of the Dead", a semi-circular, open cylinder projecting outwards, from which there is a view into the expanse of the desert, remain of the dramatic sweep of the first model. The most notable feature of the complex are the three domes over the entrance hall cut out of one of the wings, the ceiling of which is as high as the building in which it is located. Mendelsohn commented, "We look down here over villages that are three thousand years old, or is it already six thousand, who knows? Everywhere, little stone houses with dome roofs. Hence, I adopted the form of the dome here."

The hospital is made of reinforced concrete clad in vertical panels of artificial stone. Mendelsohn's Hadassah complex looks cubic and hard, "on a large scale and with

The entire complex: in front, the nursing school, and to the left, the Nathan Ratnoff school

great freedom. With balanced proportions and a sort of unpretentious simplicity, with a logic that I seek very early on and which is always my goal." (Mendelsohn)

The interior was designed by Mendelsohn's office – from the extravagant lighting through to the geometrical pattern of the flooring and the furniture, all the way to the ashtrays and vases. In terms of the interior design, Mendelsohn oriented himself to the wishes and the habits of the users, and in Palestine they were, for the most part, European immigrants.

At the same time, in 1937/38, Erich Mendelsohn built a second large hospital in Palestine: the Government Hospital in Haifa. Mendelsohn was commissioned in this case directly by the British High Commissioner Arthur Wauchope, who knew him from London, admired his architecture. Mendelsohn was, however, never able to develop a rapport with Wauchope's successor after 1938, and his dream of becoming the chief architect of Palestine was dashed.

for vines!

venting here at in all patients floors

or better as individual! screen boxes in metal

1946–1950▸Maimonides-Hospital
San Francisco, California, USA

The southern façade in a sketch (opposite page) and in a photograph from 1950

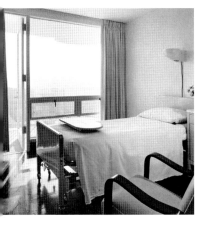

The patients' rooms were flooded with light, but protected from the strong rays of the sun by balconies that projected far beyond the façade of the building.

The Maimonides Hospital, now the Women's Health Center at the Medical Center of Mount Zion, was built for the chronically ill, hence, very few rooms were required for diagnosis and treatment. Mendelsohn located them, along with the administrative offices, in two low-rise buildings that protect the long building site, which was only 98.5 feet wide, from the noise of the street. He set the nine-storey main building, flanked by two gardens, at the centre, where it fills the entire width of the lot. It is made of reinforced concrete and its supporting walls form an "H" in plan. All the patients' rooms are located on the sunny southern side; the front sides are windowless, the wall between the patients´ rooms and the corridor forms the "cross member" of the "H". Hence, the long northern side is not a supporting wall either. It has horizontal and vertical bands of windows, and round windows at the corridors, lifts and stairways. The southern side was divided into large window areas. For protection against the sun, the outer walls were so far recessed, that deep, interconnected balconies were created. The rhythm of the façade results from four rows of semi-circular balconies swinging out one above the other. Only the first floor had a different design; it was where the treatment rooms and lounges were located. The hospital, which was planned in 1946, begun in 1948, and dedicated in 1950, was altered by the owner as early as 1952. The four-bed rooms were converted into six-bed rooms by incorporating the recessed balconies. The new external wall constructed at this time had smaller windows.

1946–1950·Synagogue B'Nai Amoona

St. Louis, Missouri, USA

The Ark is located in a niche on the front wall of the sanctuary, which extends on across the entire ceiling of the sanctuary.

Mendelsohn did not receive his licence as an architect until five years after arriving in the United States. His hope of becoming a professor at one of the major universities, and having enough time to practise architecture on the side, was never fulfilled. His contract as a lecturer at the University of California in Berkeley was not as prestigious or as influential as the positions held by Gropius at Harvard or Mies in Chicago. But from 1946 on, Mendelsohn did find a new field of activity: building synagogues.

After the Second World War, numerous synagogues were built in the United States. The four synagogues built by Erich Mendelsohn, along with four others he designed, but which were never built, and his writings on the subject proved highly influential. Features such as flexible floor plans and his modern, simple and yet symbolically rich language of forms were often emulated. It is important to remember that the layout of a synagogue is not predetermined by any fixed typology. The building only needs to be functional, the sanctity of the sanctuary results from the activities that take place in it. A synagogue is not only a house of prayer, it is also the social centre for the congregation that uses it in many ways, including as a school. In his designs, Mendelsohn had to provide for the sanctuary, the secular assembly room and the school.

Mendelsohn was well known in Jewish circles in America as the architect of the Hadassah University Hospital, the construction of which had been financed mainly by American donations. People in St. Louis were also familiar with Mendelsohn because of the MoMA exhibition shown there in 1944. In spring 1946, he presented the first draft of his design to the congregation, construction was begun in summer 1948, and the dedication took place in 1950.

The U-shaped building is laid out around an inner courtyard, with a covered promenade shielding the open face from the street. The two wings, each of different width and height, house classrooms, offices and an assembly hall. The sanctuary, which towers over this complex, is laid out as an elongated rectangle and ensconced under a parabolic roof that starts on the ground and extends far beyond the foyer on the other side. Set into the front wall there is a niche for the Ark crowned by the Ten Commandments. This indentation is continued on upwards and over the entire length of the middle aisle as a raised central strip. Windows are set into the gap created by the two different levels of the roof. This allows light from the west to shine into the room from up above and onto the Commandments at the centre. By means of folding walls, the sanctuary can be enlarged (for more visitors on the high holidays) to include the adjacent foyer. Similarly, it is also possible to combine the foyer with the adjacent assembly hall. The idea of a flexible layout was not new, but Mendelsohn was the first to apply it to the construction of American synagogues in the twentieth century.

Opposite page:
View of the temple, with its striking extended roof, from the inner courtyard

1946 – 1953 · Park Synagogue
Cleveland, Ohio, USA

Opposite page:
The western point of the synagogue complex,
which is laid out in a triangle

Right:
Conceptual sketch for the sanctuary

The foyer of the sanctuary

In Cleveland, the sanctuary, as American reformed Jews generally refer to the room where prayer services are held, is a domed hall. The congregation had bought a building site on a hill outside of the city, and Mendelsohn adapted his design to the topography. He situated a flat building with a triangular floor plan on the wedge-shaped site at the cusp of the hill, the low, copper-clad dome at the centre of the complex can be seen from afar. Like the rest of the complex, it is made of reinforced concrete. The point at which the walls of the building come together at the sharpest angle resembles the rounded off bow of a ship, a chapel for weekday services is located there, while the foyer is in the wider part of the building, on the other side of the dome, but can be combined with the domed hall as needed. Round windows provide illumination. Erich Mendelsohn opened up the ground floor area of the domed hall by installing a band of windows interrupted only by narrow supports. A canopy – reminiscent of a tent in the desert – is stretched over the pulpit. The school wing almost seems like a later addition, since it transforms the wedge-shaped building into one with three wings and an inner courtyard.

Mendelsohn's American synagogues display very different, but always simple, geometric forms, the symbolic meaning of which is emphasized by abstaining from the use of ornamentation. Examples of this are the dome that provides a protective shield over the congregation, the tent over the pulpit reminiscent of wandering in the desert, and the twelve steps that led up to the Holy Ark (in St. Paul).

1947–1951 ▸ Russell House
San Francisco, California, USA

View of San Francisco Bay and the Golden Gate Bridge from the bay windows

Mendelsohn's only residential building in America was erected in the wealthy San Francisco neighbourhood of Pacific Heights. The Russell House has a flat roof and two wings forming an "L". The smaller one is set at a right angle to the street and contains the kitchen, utility, children's and maids rooms as well as an underground garage. The main wing is parallel to the street of the highest ridge on the property that slopes steeply towards San Francisco Bay. It rests on slender steel pillars, so that the Golden Gate Bridge can be seen underneath it from the entrance to the property. The living room, dining room and fireplace area are located on the first floor, and the bedrooms on the second. The southern façade, overlooking the street, is almost fully glazed. The first floor has a terrace with balustrades that curve outwards. The balustrade in front of the second floor and the wooden solar protection extending outwards make the building seem even lighter and airier.

At the back of the house, the first floor is recessed in order to provide room for a deeper terrace, thus making the upper level look like it is floating, when viewed from below. The solution for the corner on the second floor is spectacular: a glass bay projecting as three quarters of a circle held in place by extended floor and ceiling slabs. The few remaining windows in the upper floor are also curved. Otherwise, this floor is more like a closed box; its walls are clad in horizontal layers of Californian redwood, like the rest of the house. The rooms in the interior can be opened up to each other by sliding back walls. Mendelsohn also designed all of the furniture. Although the building had been planned since 1947, construction did not begin until 1950, and a year later the house was ready for occupancy. The first resident, Madeleine H. Russell, lived there for more than fifty years. The house has been, for the most part, preserved in its original state.

Opposite page:
Seen from the back, the upper floor of the house seems to be suspended in air.

Life and Work

The dates cited are those on which planning began and not when the buildings were begun or completed.

1887 ▸ Erich Mendelsohn is born as the fourth of five children of a Jewish merchant and a milliner on 21 March in Allenstein (East Prussia, now Olsztyn, Poland).

1906 ▸ After his final school exams, Mendelsohn begins training as a merchant in Berlin, but moves to Munich after a short time in order to study economics.

1908–1910 ▸ Studies architecture at the Technische Hochschule Charlottenburg (now the Technical University of Berlin). Mendelsohn also pursues an interest in oil painting and printmaking.

1910–1912 ▸ Continues his studies at the Technical University of Munich under Theodor Fischer. Receives a diploma.

1911
Jewish Cemetery, Chapel, Allenstein, Germany (now Olsztyn, Poland)

1912–1914 ▸ Freelance architect in Munich. Earns his living designing posters and programmes, stage sets, costumes, and furniture. First architectural sketches.

1914 ▸ Mendelsohn, initially deferred from military service because of poor eyesight, moves to Berlin.

1915 ▸ Voluntary training as a medic for the Red Cross.
Marriage to the cellist Luise Maas on 6 October.
Villa Karl Becker, renovation, Chemnitz, Germany (never realized)

1916 ▸ Birth of daughter Esther.

1917 ▸ Military service on the Russian front where he makes numerous architectural sketches.

1918 ▸ Transfer to the French front.
On 7 November, the day of his return to Berlin,

Mendelsohn opens an architectural office in the Westend.
Einstein Tower, Potsdam, Germany

1919 ▸ In January and February Mendelsohn holds eight lectures on "Architecture" in Molly Philippson's salon in Berlin. His ideas attract a number of future clients among the listeners. Exhibition under the title "Architecture in Iron and Concrete" at the Galerie Paul Cassirer, Berlin. The exhibition is later shown in six other German cities.
Gottower Strasse Estate, Luckenwalde, Germany
Hat Factory Herrmann & Co, factory building, Luckenwalde, Germany

1920 ▸ Special issue of the Dutch architectural magazine *Wendingen* on Mendelsohn.
Lecture tour to Amsterdam, Den Haag and Rotterdam.
New façade for the administrative headquarters of Hausleben-Versicherung in Berlin, Germany

1921 ▸ Loss of his left eye to cancer.
Hat Factory Steinberg, Herrmann & Co, Luckenwalde, Germany
Rudolf Mosse Printing and Publishing Company Building, Berlin, Germany
Skyscraper on Kemperplatz, competition entry, Berlin, Germany (never realized)
Double Villa on Karolingerplatz, Berlin, Germany

1922
Seidenhaus Weichmann, Gleiwitz, Germany (now Gliwice, Poland)
Meyer-Kauffmann Textile Factory, Wüstegiersdorf, Germany (now Glouszyca Górna, Poland)

1923 ▸ Travels to Palestine. Project for a large power plant, a satellite town on Mount Carmel and a commercial centre in Haifa (First Prize in a competition, together with Richard Neutra), never realized.
Villa Sternefeld, Berlin, Germany
Furrier C. A. Herpich & Sons, Berlin, Germany

1924 ▸ Travels to the United States, first meeting with Frank Lloyd Wright.
Co-founder of the later very influential architects' organization *Der Ring*.

Erich Mendelsohn, 1930

Louise Mendelsohn

1925 ► First of three trips to the Soviet Union.
*Lodge of the Three Patriarchs, Tilsit, Germany
(now Sovietsk, Russia)
The Red Flag Textile Factory, Leningrad (now St
Petersburg), Russia (only partially realized)
Schocken Department Store, Nuremberg, Germany
Cohen & Epstein Department Store, renovation
and expansion, Duisburg, Germany*

1926 ► *America Bilderbuch eines Architekten*
(America. An Architect's Album) published by
Rudolf Mosse Publishing Company.
*Schocken Department Store, Stuttgart, Germany
Country House Bejach, Berlin-Steinstücken,
Germany*

1927
*Rudolf Mosse Printing and Publishing Company
Building, boilerhouse, Berlin, Germany
Deukon House, renovation and expansion, Berlin,
Germany
Petersdorff Department Store, Breslau, Germany
(now Wrocław, Poland)
Jewish Cemetery, Königsberg, Germany (now
Kaliningrad, Russia)
Woga Complex with the Universum Cinema,
Berlin, Germany*

1928
*Rudolf Mosse Pavilion ("Pressa"), Cologne,
Germany (temporary exhibition building)
Schocken Department Store, Chemnitz, Germany
Mendelsohn House (Haus Am Rupenhorn),
Berlin, Germany
German Metal Workers' Federation Building,
Berlin, Germany*

1929 ► *Russland, Europa, Amerika. Ein
architektonischer Querschnitt* (Russia, Europe,
America. An Architectural Cross Section)
published by Rudolf Mosse Publishing Company.
Mendelsohn wins the shared First Prize in the
prestigious competition for a high-rise at the
Friedrichstrasse station in Berlin.

1930
Jewish Youth Centre, Essen, Germany

1931 ► Named as Member of the Prussian
Academy of the Arts in Berlin (excluded again in
1933).
Competition entry for the Palace of the Soviets in
Moscow.
Columbus House, Berlin, Germany

1932
*Dobloug Gaarden Department Store, Oslo,
Norway (executed by Rudolf Emanuel Jacobsen)
Bachner Department Store, Mährisch
Ostrau/Ostrava, Czechoslovakia (now the Czech
Republic)*

1933 ► Mendelsohn emigrates with his wife and
daughter to Amsterdam and then to London.
Mediterranean Academy Project in Cavalaire near
St. Tropez on the Côte d'Azur.
Mendelsohn becomes the senior partner in an
architectural office with the 33-year-old, Russian-
English architect Serge Chermayeff in London.
*Nimmo House (Shurb's Wood), Chalfont St.
Giles, Great Britain (with Chermayeff)
De La Warr Pavilion, Bexhill-on-Sea, Great
Britain (with Chermayeff)*

1934
*Cohen House, Chelsea (London), Great Britain
(with Chermayeff)
Weizmann House, Rehovoth, Palestine (now Israel)*

*Schocken House and Library, Jerusalem, Palestine
(now Israel)
Hadassah University Hospital, Mount Scopus,
Jerusalem, Palestine (now Israel)*

1935 ► Mendelsohn opens a second office in
Jerusalem.
Joint project with Chermayeff, renovation of the
White City area near London.
*W. & A. Gilbey Building, London, Great Britain
(with Chermayeff)
Max Pine Boys' Trade School, Tel Aviv,
Palestine (now Israel, with Chermayeff)*

1936 ► Mendelsohn and Chermayeff end their
partnership.
*Ludwig Tietz Trade School, Jagur, Palestine
(now Israel)
Anglo-Palestinian Bank (now National Bank of
Israel), Jerusalem, Palestine (now Israel)*

1937
Government Hospital, Haifa, Palestine (now Israel)

1938 ► Mendelsohn becomes a British citizen.

Erich Mendelsohn at his drawing table, 1940

aniel Wolf Research Laboratory, Rehovoth, Palestine (now Israel)

939 ▶ Mendelsohn named a Fellow of the Royal Institute of British Architects, changes his first name to "Eric" and moves to Jerusalem in the summer.

940
Agricultural School in Rehovoth, Palestine (now Israel)

941 ▶ Mendelsohn emigrates to the United States. He spends three months travelling throughout the country by car, after which his New York colleague Ely Jacques Kahn provides him with a room in his architectural office. The Mendelsohns live with friends on a farm in Croton-on-Hudson near New York until 1945. In December the MoMA shows an individual exhibition of his work.

942 ▶ For *Fortune* magazine in New York, Mendelsohn develops fantasy designs for the post-war period: an "Airborne Community", a central metropolitan airport, the main street in a major city, etc.

943 ▶ With a two-year grant from the Simon Guggenheim Memorial Foundation he is able to work on a book about his own architecture: "A Contemporary Philosophy of Architecture". It remains a fragment.

945 ▶ Moves to San Francisco, where he initially opens a joint office with the architects John Ekin Dinwiddie and Albert Henry Hill.

946 ▶ Mendelsohn becomes an American citizen and is granted a licence as an architect in California on 12 August.
Synagogue B'Nai Amoona, St. Louis, Missouri
Maimonides Hospital, San Francisco, California
Park Synagogue, Cleveland, Ohio

947 ▶ Awarded a tenured position at the University of California, Berkeley (until 1953).
Russell House, San Francisco, California

Frank Lloyd Wright and Erich Mendelsohn, 1947

1948
Synagogue Emanu-El, Grand Rapids, Michigan

1949 ▶ Mendelsohn wins a competition for a monument to the six million Jewish victims of National Socialism in Riverside Park, New York (never realized).

1950
Synagogue Mount Zion, St. Paul, Minnesota
Varian Associates, Offices and Laboratories, Palo Alto, California

1952
Laboratory Building for the Atomic Energy Commission of the University of California, Berkeley, California

1953 ▶ Erich Mendelsohn dies of cancer on 15 September in San Francisco. His ashes are strewn over the Pacific Ocean according to his own wishes.

Germany

NORDSEE

OSTSEE

Hamburg

Bremen

Elbe

Berlin

Oder

Hannover

Weser

Potsdam

Havel

Luckenwalde

Spree

Ruhr

Kassel

Saale

Elbe

Leipzig

Köln

Dresden

Rhein

Saale

Chemnitz

Frankfurt/Main

Main

Nürnberg

Rhein

Stuttgart

Donau

Isar

Rhein

München

World Map

GROSSBRITANNIEN
Bexhill-on-Sea

RUSSLAND
● Kaliningrad

POLEN
● Wroclaw

USA
● Cleveland
San Francisco
● St.Louis

ATLANTISCHER OZEAN

Rehovoth
ISRAEL
● Jerusalem

Great Britain
Bexhill-on-Sea
De La Warr Pavilion

Israel
Rehovoth
Weizmann House

Jerusalem
Schocken House and Library
Hadassah University Hospital

Poland
Wroclaw
Petersdorff Department Store

Russia
Kaliningrad
Jewish Cemetery

USA
San Francisco, California
Maimonides Hospital
Russell House

Cleveland, Ohio
Park Synagogue

St. Louis, Missouri
Synagogue B'Nai Amoona

Bibliography

▶ Achenbach, Sigrid (ed.). *Erich Mendelsohn 1887–1953. Ideen. Bauten. Projekte.* Exhib. cat. Kunstbibliothek Berlin. Berlin, 1987.
▶ Beyer, Oskar (ed.). *Erich Mendelsohn. Briefe eines Architekten.* Munich, 1961.
▶ Eckardt, Wolf von. *Eric Mendelsohn.* London, 1960.
▶ *Fünf Architekten aus fünf Jahrhunderten.* Exhib. cat. Kunstbibliothek Berlin. Berlin, 1976.
▶ Heinze-Mühleib, Ita. *Erich Mendelsohn. Bauten und Projekte in Palästina (1934–1941).* Munich, 1986.
▶ Huse, Norbert (ed.). *Mendelsohn. Der Einsteinturm. Die Geschichte einer Instandsetzung.* Stuttgart/Zurich, 2000.
▶ Mendelsohn, Erich. *Amerika. Bilderbuch eines Architekten.* Berlin, 1926.
▶ Mendelsohn, Erich. *Das Gesamtschaffen des Architekten. Skizzen Entwürfe, Bauten.* Berlin, 1930. (Erich Mendelsohn. *The Complete Works of the Architect: Sketches, Designs, Buildings.* Trans., Princeton, 1992.)
▶ Mendelsohn, Erich. *Neues Haus – Neue Welt.* Berlin, 1932.
▶ Mendelsohn, Erich. *Russland – Europa – Amerika. Ein architektonischer Querschnitt.* Berlin, 1929.
▶ Mendelsohn, Louise. "Biographical Note on Eric," *L'Architettura* 9, 1963, pp. 295–422.
▶ Richter, Tilo. *Erich Mendelsohns Kaufhaus Schocken. Jüdische Kulturgeschichte in Chemnitz.* Leipzig, 1998.
▶ Stephan, Regina (ed.). *Erich Mendelsohn – Gebaute Welten.* Ostfildern, 1998.
▶ Stephan, Regina. *Studien zu Waren- und Geschäftshäusern Erich Mendelsohns in Deutschland.* Munich, 1992.
▶ Whittick, Arnold. *Eric Mendelsohn.* 2nd ed., New York, 1956.
▶ Zevi, Bruno. *Erich Mendelsohn. Opera completa.* Milan, 1970. (Zevi, Bruno. *Erich Mendelsohn. The Complete Works.* Trans., Berlin, 1999.)
▶ Zevi, Bruno. *Erich Mendelsohn.* Zurich, 1983.

Credits

The Author

Arnt Cobbers studied art history, history and music before writing a dissertation on medieval church architecture. After working as an architectural critic, he is now a freelance author in Berlin. Among his many publications are books on architecture in Berlin, as well as on the work of Frank Lloyd Wright, Mies van der Rohe, Karl Friedrich Schinkel, I.M. Pei and others. He is also the editor-in-chief of the music magazine *Partituren*.